100.

YOUNG PEOPLE
and **SOCIAL CHANGE**

SOCIOLOGY *and* SOCIAL CHANGE

Series Editor: *Alan* **Warde, Lancaster University**

YOUNG PEOPLE
and SOCIAL CHANGE
Individualization *and* risk
in late modernity

Andy **Furlong** *and Fred* **Cartmel**

Open University Press
Buckingham · Philadelphia

Open University Press
Celtic Court
22 Ballmoor
Buckingham
MK18 1XW

and
1900 Frost Road, Suite 101
Bristol, PA 19007, USA

First Published 1997

Copyright © Andy Furlong and Fred Cartmel 1997

A catalogue record of this book is available from the British Library

ISBN 0 335 19464 8 (pb) 0 335 19465 6 (hb)

Library of Congress Cataloging-in-Publication Data
Furlong, Andy.
    Young people and social change: individualization and risk in
late modernity /Andy Furlong and Fred Cartmel.
        p. cm. — (Sociology and social change)
    Includes bibliographical references (p.) and index.
    ISBN 0–335–19465–6 (hard). — ISBN 0–335–19464–8 (pbk.)
    1. Youth—Great Britain—Social conditions. 2. Great Britain—
Social conditions—1956– I. Cartmel, Fred, 1952– . II. Title.
III. Series.
HQ799.G7F86 1997
305.235'0941—dc21

96–45149
CIP

Typeset by Graphicraft Typesetters Ltd., Hong Kong
Printed in Great Britain by Biddles Ltd, Guildford and King's Lynn

Contents

List *of* figures *and* tables

Figures

Tables

Series editor's preface

In response to perceived major transformations, social theorists have offered forceful, appealing, but contrasting accounts of the predicament of contemporary Western societies. Key themes emerging have been frequently condensed into terms like post-modernism, post-modernity, risk society, disorganized capitalism, the information society. These have important and widespread ramifications for the analysis of all areas of social life and personal well-being. The speculative and general theses proposed by social theorists must be subjected to evaluation in the light of the best available evidence if they are to serve as guides to understanding and modifying social arrangements. One purpose of sociology, among other social sciences, is to marshal the information necessary to estimate the extent and direction of social change. This series is designed to make such information, and debates about social change, accessible.

The focus of the series is the critical appraisal of general, substantive theories through examination of their applicability to different institutional areas of contemporary societies. Each book introduces key current debates and surveys of existing sociological argument and research about institutional complexes in advanced societies. The integrating theme of the series is the evaluation of the extent of social change, particularly in the last twenty years. Each author offers explicit and extended evaluation of the pace and direction of social change in their chosen area.

Andy Furlong and Fred Cartmel present an authoritative overview of very recent sociological evidence about the contemporary transition to adulthood. They chart some sharp and significant changes in the nature and experience of the transition which have occurred since the 1970s. As the duration of the transition has lengthened and the apparent alternative routes increased in number, the process has seemed to become more hazardous and uncertain. For the young people involved choices appear to have multiplied and the sense of responsibility for success or failure to have become even more a personal and individual matter. Yet objective constraints imposed by entrenched social structural divisions of class and gender operate much as before. The authors examine the new scenarios and old barriers that operate in various spheres of the social life – including education, labour markets, consumption and politics. Enriched by their own original research on youth, they document the circumstances of the young while simultaneously critically evaluating influential theoretical accounts of the process of individualization associated with Beck and Giddens. A bold general thesis, supported by a fresh and wide-ranging account of the current experience of youth, serves to distinguish lucidly between aspects of change and continuity. This book is a fine contribution to the sociological analysis of contemporary social and institutional change.

Alan Warde

Acknowledgements

A number of people have made valuable comments on various drafts of this book and have supplied us with useful literature and statistics. We are especially grateful to our friend and colleague Andy Biggart who read the entire manuscript, pointed us in the direction of additional literature and questioned our interpretation of the data at various stages. In addition, Lynne Bennie responded to our request for further information on young people's political behaviour by compiling tables from the British Election Survey, for which we are especially grateful given the lack of published material on young people's political behaviour. Others read and commented on selected chapters; in this context we would like to express our thanks to Michéle Burman, Katie Buston, Bob Coles, Paul Littlewood, Steve Miles and Patrick West. Obviously we bear responsibility for any misinterpretations. We are also grateful to the Department of Sociology at the University of Glasgow for the facilities which have been made available as well as to the staff in the University Library. The Centre for Educational Sociology at Edinburgh University kindly provided access to the Scottish Young People's Survey. Finally, in different ways, Jacinta Evans and Justin Vaughan at Open University Press and the series editor, Alan Warde made valuable contributions to the final product.

Andy Furlong and Fred Cartmel
University of Glasgow

List *of* abbreviations

BTEC   Business and Technical Education Council
CND   Campaign for Nuclear Disarmament
ESRC   Economic and Social Research Council
GCSE   General Certificate of Secondary Education
GDP   Gross Domestic Product
GHQ   General Health Questionnaire
GNP   Gross National Product
GNVQ   General and National Vocational Council
NVQ   National Vocational Qualification
SYPS   Scottish Young People's Survey
TVEI   Technical and Vocational Educational Initiative
YCS   Youth Cohort Study
YOP   Youth Opportunities Programme
YT   Youth Training
YTS   Youth Training Scheme

1 *The* risk society

Human beings may act under the belief that they are productive, free
and equal when the opposite is the case. Defining their activity as
they comprehend it will lead us to misconstrue their act . . . Human
beings can only act toward the world on the basis of some
'understanding' but it does not follow from this that their activity, or
the world, possesses the character which they 'understand' it to have.

(Lichtman 1970: 77, quoted in Rubenstein 1981: 82)

Introduction

The life experiences of young people in modern industrialized societies
have changed quite significantly over the last two decades. These changes
affect relationships with family and friends, experiences in education and
the labour market, leisure and lifestyles and the ability to become established
as independent young adults. Many of these changes are a direct result of
the restructuring of the labour market, of an increased demand for educated
workers, flexible specialization in the workplace and of social policies which
have extended the period in which young people remain dependent on their
families. As a consequence of these changes, young people today have to
negotiate a set of risks which were largely unknown to their parents; this is
true irrespective of social background or gender. Moreover, as many of these
changes have come about within a relatively short period of time, points of
reference which previously helped smooth processes of social reproduction
have become obscure. In turn, increased uncertainty can be seen as a source
of stress and vulnerability.

On a theoretical level, these changes have been expressed in a number of
ways with sociologists holding different opinions about whether they signify
the beginning of a new era, just as significant as the transition from medieval
to modern society, or whether they represent developments within modernity.
At one end of the spectrum, post-modernists such as Lyotard (1984) and
Baudrillard (1988) argue that we have entered a new, post-modern, epoch in
which structural analysis has lost its validity. In post-modern societies it is
no longer seen as appropriate to apply grand theories to the study of social
life. Patterns of behaviour and individual life chances have lost their predictability and post-modernism involves a new and much more diverse set of
lifestyles. The validity of a science of the social is rejected, along with the
usefulness of key explanatory variables such as class and gender. As Lash and
Urry suggest, for post-modernists, 'all that is solid about organised capitalism,

class, industry, cities, collectivity, nation-states, even the world, melts into air'
(1987: 313). Other theorists have been more cautious in their interpretation
of the changes and have used terms like 'high modernity', 'late modernity'
(Giddens 1990, 1991) or 'reflexive modernisation' (Lash 1992) to draw attention to the far reaching implications of recent socioeconomic change, at the
same time as expressing the view that, as yet, these changes do not represent
an epochal shift.[1] This is a view with which we concur.

There is little doubt in our minds that radical social changes have
occurred, yet we are extremely sceptical of the validity of post-modernist theories. Modernity has always involved differentiation, a plurality of lifeworlds
(Berger *et al.* 1974), a weakening of communal regulation and a sense of
uncertainty (Durkheim 1947); indeed, the weakening of traditional ties, the
depersonalization of relations and the growing obscurity of factors which
structure patterns of exploitation in advanced capitalism were identified by
the founding fathers of sociology. While structures have fragmented, changed
their form and become increasingly obscure, we suggest that life chances and
experiences can still largely be predicted using knowledge of individual's
locations within social structures; class and gender divisions remain central
to an understanding of life experiences.

In this book we provide empirical evidence to support our argument
that concepts which have long been central to sociological analysis still provide a foundation on which we can develop an understanding of processes of
social reproduction in the modern world. Nevertheless, we suggest that Beck
and Giddens have been successful in identifying processes of individualization
and risk which characterize late modernity and which have implications for
lived experiences. In particular, we suggest that life in late modernity revolves
around an epistemological fallacy: although social structures, such as class,
continue to shape life chances, these structures tend to become increasingly
obscure as collectivist traditions weaken and individualist values intensify.
As a consequence of these changes, people come to regard the social world
as unpredictable and filled with risks which can only be negotiated on an
individual level, even though chains of human interdependence (Elias 1978,
1982) remain intact.

In many respects, the study of youth provides an ideal opportunity to
examine the relevance of new social theories; if the social order has changed
and if social structures have weakened, we would expect to find evidence of
these changes among young people who are at the crossroads of the process
of social reproduction. One of the key aims of this book is to uncover evidence of the changing impact of social structures through the study of youth
in modern Britain. The central questions we seek to answer relate first to
whether the traditional parameters which were previously understood as struc-
turing the life chances and experiences of young people are still relevant.
Second, addressing issues raised by Beck (1992) and Giddens (1991), we will
examine the extent to which the terms 'individualization' and 'risk' convey
an accurate picture of the changing life contexts of the young.

We accept that the experiences of young people have changed quite radically over the last two decades, yet suggest that in the age of high modernity
life chances and processes of social reproduction remain highly structured.

We also agree that there has been a breakdown in 'ontological security' (Giddens 1991) which validates the claim that modernity, as traditionally understood, is changing.[2] It is possible to draw on a number of theorists within the late modernist tradition to understand these changes (such as Bauman 1988 and Lash 1992), but in our opinion, the ideas of Ulrich Beck which were put forward in his book *Risk Society* (1992) and those of Anthony Giddens in *Modernity and Self Identity* (1991) provide clear statements about the nature of these changes and therefore a good base for the study of young people in the late modern age. We begin this chapter with a summary of the ideas of Beck and Giddens and then start to identify some of the ways in which they can be applied to an understanding of young people in modern Britain.

Risikogesellschaft

In *Risk Society* (*Risikogesellschaft*) Beck (1992) argues that the Western world is witnessing an historical transformation. Industrial society is being replaced by a new modernity in which the old, 'scientific', world view is being challenged; predictabilities and certainties characteristic of the industrial era are threatened and a new set of risks and opportunities are brought into existence. Whereas modernity involved rationality and the belief in the potential offered by harnessing scientific knowledge, in late modernity the world is perceived as a dangerous place in which we are constantly confronted with risk. These risks include those stemming from the threat of nuclear war or environmental disasters, as well as other risks which have to be negotiated in day to day life. Indeed, according to Beck, people are progressively freed from the social networks and constraints of the old order and forced to negotiate a new set of hazards which impinge on all aspects of their day to day lives. Previous securities are broken and people's concerns start to centre upon the prevention or elimination of the risks which are systematically produced as part of modernization.

This is not to suggest that we have moved into a new era of classlessness or that people's structural locations have a limited effect on their life chances. Beck acknowledges that risks are unequally distributed within society and may be arranged in a manner which follow the inequalities characteristic of class society:

> Like wealth, risks adhere to the class pattern, only inversely: wealth accumulates at the top, risks at the bottom. To that extent, risks seem to *strengthen*, not abolish, the class society. Poverty attracts an unfortunate abundance of risks. By contrast, the wealthy (in income, power or education) can *purchase* safety and freedom from risk.
>
> (1992: 35)

Despite an unequal vulnerability to risk, Beck does suggest that class ties have weakened (at least in a subjective sense) and that in late modernity it is not always possible to predict lifestyles, political beliefs and opinions using information about occupations or family backgrounds. Indeed, Beck argues that 'people with the same income level, or to put it in the old-fashioned way, within the same "class", can or even must choose between different lifestyles, subcultures, social ties and identities' (1992: 131).

Because individual behaviour and lifestyles can no longer be predicted using concepts like social class, Beck describes the new epoch as 'capitalism *without* classes' (1992: 88). Individualized lifestyles come into being in which people are forced to put themselves at the centre of their plans and reflexively construct their social biographies. The workplace becomes less of an arena for conflicts, and ascribed social differences such as gender and racial inequalities come to assume a greater significance. In all aspects of their lives, people have to choose between different options, including the social groups with which they wish to be identified, and temporary allegiances are formed in respect to particular issues. People may join a number of social and political groups whose aims appear to clash; they may join a trade union, for example, and vote Conservative, yet Beck regards these various allegiances as representing pragmatic responses by individuals in the struggle for survival in the risk society.

While we agree with Beck that subjective dimensions of class have weakened and that lifestyles have become increasingly individualized, it is important to stress that we are not arguing that class has weakened as a predictor of individual life chances. It is also important to be clear about Beck's view of the ongoing nature of social divisions which continue to shape life chances; he is not suggesting that social inequalities disappear or weaken within the new modernity. Social inequality continues to exert a powerful hold over people's lives, but increasingly does so at the level of the individual rather than the group or class. Beck admits that within Western societies social inequalities display 'an amazing stability' (1992: 91) and that empirical research is unlikely to uncover significant changes. 'Income inequalities, the structure of the division of labour, and the basic determinants of wage labour have, after all, remained relatively unchanged' (1992: 92), although there has been a weakening of class identities and the individualization of lifestyles.

Thus while structures of inequality remain deeply entrenched, in our view one of the most significant features of late modernity is the epistemological fallacy: the growing disjuncture between objective and subjective dimensions of life. People's life chances remain highly structured at the same time as they increasingly seek solutions on an individual, rather than a collective basis. Beck argues that in late modernity, risks have become 'individualized' and people increasingly regard setbacks and crises as individual shortcomings, rather than as outcomes of processes which are beyond their personal control. Unemployment, for example, may be seen as a consequence of a lack of skills on the part of the individual, rather than as the result of a general decline in demand for labour stemming from a world economic recession. Similarly, problems faced by school-leavers in less advantaged areas may be seen as a reflection of their lack of qualifications rather than a consequence of material circumstances and the lack of compensatory mechanisms within the school. The individualization of risk may mean that situations which would once have led to a call for political action are now interpreted as something which can only be solved on an individual level through personal action. As a consequence of these changes, Beck argues that an increase in social inequality may be associated with an intensifica- tion of individualization as more people are placed in unpleasant situations which they interpret as being due, in part, to their own failures. In the risk society, individual subjectivity becomes an important force, a force which is often more significant than class positions.

The social processes identified by Beck have received broad support in the work of Anthony Giddens (1990, 1991), although there are significant differences which we highlight in the concluding chapter. Giddens argues that the age of high modernity is characterized by a risk culture in so far as people today are subject to uncertainties which were not part of day to day life for previous generations. Within this risk culture, the self is reflexively created as people are forced to interpret a diversity of experiences in a way which helps them establish a coherent biography. Thus Giddens argues that people have to accept the central part played by risk in their lives which in- volves acknowledging 'that no aspects of our activities follow a pre-ordained course, and all are open to contingent happenings' (1991: 28). Furthermore,

> living in the 'risk society' means living with a calculative attitude to the open possibilities of action, positive and negative, with which, as individuals and globally, we are confronted in a continuous way in our contemporary social existence.
>
> (1991: 28)

Unlike post-modern perspectives, the interpretation of high modernity presented by Beck and Giddens and their view of changes in the balance of the relationship between individual and society does not mean that people are free to re-create the world in increasingly diverse forms. Individuals are dependent on the labour market, education and regulations which govern many different aspects of their social existence and this, in turn, leads to new forms of standardization. For Giddens, modernity 'produces difference, exclusion and marginalization' (1991: 6). Diversification involves the emer- gence of new experiences and trajectories, but does not involve a process of equalization nor does it dilute the nature of class-based inequalities on an objective level. Class still has an impact on people's life chances, but as a res- ult of the fragmentation of social structures, collective identities have weak- ened. In this context we will argue that processes of diversification within the school and the labour market may obscure underlying class relationships and may provide the impression of greater equality and individualization without actually providing anything of substance – a process which we refer to as the epistemological fallacy of late modernity.

Growing up in the risk society

In this book we describe some of the ways in which social changes occur- ring over the last two to three decades have led to a heightened sense of risk and a greater individualization of experiences among young people. Despite the far reaching implications of social change, we will argue that there are powerful sources of continuity; young people's experiences continue to be shaped by class and gender. We also highlight the maintenance of inequalities associated with 'race', while recognizing that experiences of different ethnic groups can be quite distinct. In our view, 'race' is a socially constructed category but one which is central to the understanding of structured inequalities within advanced capitalist societies. The analysis of the impact of 'race' on the life experiences of young people is complex because many of the disadvantages faced by members of ethnic minorities are a consequence of their position within the class structure, rather than being a feature of racial exclusion.[3] In this respect, we agree with Miles that 'racism is always part of a wider structure of class disadvantage and exclusion' (1989: 9).

Young people today are growing up in a different world to that experienced by previous generations – changes which are significant enough to merit a reconceptualization of youth transitions and processes of social reproduction. Metaphorically, the old model of social reproduction, frequently described in terms of trajectories (Banks *et al.* 1992) can be viewed in terms of railway journeys (Roberts 1995). Within the school, young people join trains which are bound for different destinations. The trains they board are determined by factors like social class, gender and educational attainment. Once the train journey has begun, opportunities to switch destinations are limited; it may be possible to upgrade the class of ticket or disembark at an intermediary station, but given that the trains follow different tracks, there are few real chances to change direction. As a result of spending long periods of time in the company of other passengers, a certain camaraderie develops; people become aware of their common experiences and destinations. They may develop an affinity with fellow passengers and start to develop a comfortable familiarity with their own particular train. Conversely, if they become dissatisfied with aspects of their journey, they may recognize that a change of direction can only be achieved through collective action.

Whereas train journeys may have provided a good metaphor for processes of social reproduction and the experiences of youth in the 1960s and 1970s, we can best describe the changes occurring over the last twenty years in terms of the wholesale closure of the railways. With the absence of trains, the journey from class of origin to class of destination is now undertaken by car (Roberts 1995). While trains must remain on a predetermined set of rails, the car driver is able to select his or her route from a vast number of alternatives. Unlike the railway passenger, the individual car driver is constantly faced with a series of decisions relating to routes which will take them from their point of origin to their destination. They can take the motorway, follow A roads, stick to minor roads, scenic routes, or can follow any combination of these routes. At many junctions, they can switch routes and may decide to change roads due to difficulties in making progress on roads previously selected.

Throughout the journey, most drivers maintain the impression of having some control over the speed and comfort of their journeys. They are able to monitor the progress of other road users, may come to hear of short-cuts through access to useful information networks and perhaps develop advanced driving techniques. The experience of driving one's own car rather than travelling as a passenger on public transport leads to the impression that individual skills and decisions are crucial to the determination of outcomes. Through all of this, drivers frequently have some awareness that fellow travellers are making their journeys in different types of cars; they may be passed by high performance cars like Jaguars and Porsches and in turn they may frequently overtake Ladas and Skodas. But under certain road conditions, such as congested junctions, even the Lada driver may find an opportunity to overtake a Porsche.

With the impression of having control over the timing and routing of their journeys and with the experience of passing other motorists, what many of the drivers fail to realize is that the type of car which they have been allocated at the start of the journey is the most significant predictor of the ultimate outcome. Those with inferior cars find themselves spending significant periods off the road, while those driving high performance vehicles are able to take advantage of stretches of open road.

In other words, in the modern world young people face new risks and opportunities, the traditional links between the family, school and work seem to have weakened as young people embark on journeys into adulthood which involve a wide variety of routes, many of which appear to have uncertain outcomes. But the greater range of opportunities available helps to obscure the extent to which existing patterns of inequality are simply being reproduced in different ways. Moreover, because there are a much greater range of pathways to choose from, young people may develop the impression that their own route is unique and that the risks they face are to be overcome as individuals rather than as members of a collectivity.

In our view then, the risk society is not a classless society, but a society in which the old social cleavages associated with class and gender remain intact; on an objective level, changes in the distribution of risk have been minimal. However, subjective feelings of risk have become a much more significant feature of young people's lives and this has implications for their experiences and lifestyles. With traditional social divisions having become obscure, subjective risks stem from the perceived lack of collective tradition and security. Whereas subjective understandings of the social world were once shaped by class, gender and neighbourhood relations, today everything is presented as a possibility. The maintenance of traditional opportunity structures combined with subjective 'disembedding' (Giddens 1991) is a constant source of frustration and stress for today's youth.

The idea that perceptions of risk are culturally constructed and that there is an inevitable mismatch between objective risks and subjective perceptions of risk is controversial. Reports by the Royal Society have stressed the importance of developing scientific methods which bridge the gap between objective and perceived risk (Adams 1995). Yet Adams (1995) suggests that people's perceptions of the risks involved in different types of behaviour are socially constructed and affected by experiences and norms associated with their social groups. Applying for a place at university, for example, may be perceived as risky by a young person from a lower working-class family, whereas a young person with similar qualifications from an advantaged family may take their acceptance for granted. Similarly, this mismatch between subjective and objective dimensions of risk is reflected in reactions to the use of illegal drugs by young people; socially accepted drugs like alcohol pose far greater health risks.

Change in the economic order, the dismantling of Fordist social structures, the extension of education and the associated demand for credentials mean that in late modernity individuals are increasingly held accountable for their own fates. Individual accountability and achievement are values which are constantly reinforced by the school and the media, yet in reality individuals often remain powerless. The combined forces of individual responsibility and accountability, on the one hand, and vulnerability and lack of control on the other, leads to a heightened sense of risk and insecurity. Conditions of doubt penetrate all aspects of social life and self identity becomes fragile and subject to constant reinterpretation (Giddens 1991). For Beck and Giddens, this constant reinterpretation of identity signifies that life has become a 'reflexive project'; individuals are constantly forced to reconstruct their biographies in the light of changing experiences.

In the space of one generation there have been some radical changes to the typical experiences of British young people; patterns of schooling today are very different to what they were in the 1970s and the youth labour market has changed in such a way that it would be almost unrecognizable to members of previous generations. Young people from all social classes tend to remain in full-time education until a later age and higher education is becoming a mass experience rather than the preserve of a small elite. Education is increasingly packaged as a consumer product, performance league tables encourage parents to shop around for the best school for their children, while the growing range of educational credentials and courses may lead young people to treat services as products. In Chapter 2 we provide an overview of changing educational experiences and argue that despite some convergence in experiences, many forms of differentiation still exist. Although we identify some sources of individualization within the school which have an impact on young people's experiences, we argue that the traditional determinants of educational success still have a powerful affect on educational outcomes.

Over the last two decades labour market entry has become much more difficult and unemployment has become a typical part of labour market transitions for all young people, including university graduates. In Chapter 3 we describe the main changes in the youth labour market and highlight changes in the school to work transition. We suggest that collectivized transitions characteristic of a Fordist society have become much rarer as young people make transitions to a highly differentiated skill market as opposed to a relatively undifferentiated labour market. While school to work transitions have become more protracted and have increased in complexity, we argue that the essential predictability of transitions has been maintained. However, as a result of the diversity of routes, young people are faced with an increasing range of options which force them to engage with the likely consequences of their actions on a subjective level. In other words, while labour market outcomes are best described in terms of continuity rather than change, young people face these routes with a growing sense of unease and insecurity.

Along with the protraction of the school to work transition, there has been an extension to the period in which young people remain in a state of semi-dependency. Young people remain dependent on their families for longer periods of time and it has become more difficult for them to make successful domestic and housing transitions (Coles 1995; Jones 1995). While we argue that domestic and housing transitions are still strongly affected by class and gender (Chapter 4), it is suggested that changes in the sequencing of the three transitions (school to work transitions, domestic transitions and housing transitions) have led to weakening family ties. In turn, other influences, such as peer groups and the media, have become stronger. These changes have implications for behaviour and experiences in other dimensions of life.

In the age of high modernity, as subjective class affiliations, family ties and traditional expectations weaken, consumption and lifestyles have become central to the process of identity construction. Changing lifestyles and leisure experiences are discussed in Chapter 5. In this context we note that some commentators have argued style and consumption have become more important than class in the shaping of young people's lives (Featherstone 1991; Abma 1992). We disagree with this position. Although lifestyles and youth cultures are no longer shaped by social class, consumption and style are central to the lived experience of young people who are required to act as consumers in many different dimensions of life. Yet as Bauman (1988) suggests, consumption, accountability and personal responsibility are sources of stress and anxiety; thus the increased sense of personal risk which we see as impinging on young people's lives in a variety of contexts can be regarded as a product of the consumer society.

The increasing stresses and strains of modern life and their impact on young people's health are examined in Chapter 6. We suggest that as individuals are made to feel more responsible for life events, uncertainty and risk have taken their toll on young people's mental health. The incidence of mental illness, eating disorders, suicide and attempted suicide have increased as young people develop a sense of having 'no future' (West and Sweeting 1996). These trends are also affected by an increasing isolation from adult worlds. While risk-taking has always been a feature of young lives, longer transitions have led to a greater vulnerability to risk, including those which stem from involvement or vulnerability to criminal activities (Chapter 7). Domestic and work commitments have long been associated with a reduction in risk-taking activities and there is evidence that protracted transitions mean young people remain vulnerable for longer periods. To steal a buzzword from the Labour Party, young people are being denied the chance to become 'stakeholders' in their society and in turn they look for alternative sources of satisfaction, some of which carry health risks or make them more vulnerable to police surveillance and arrest.

The weakening of the traditional bonds of family and class, together with an individualization of experiences, personal risk and global insecurity can also be seen as leading to a weakening of traditional political affiliations (Chapter 8). In recent years, a number of sociologists have questioned the continued relevance of social class for an understanding of the distribution of life chances in modern Britain (e.g. Pahl 1989, 1993; Goldthorpe and Marshall 1992). We suggest that if class is 'ceasing to do any useful work for sociology', as Pahl (1989: 710) maintains, then class analysis should be at its weakest when applied to the study of youth. In particular, changes in the subjective understanding of class have implications for young people's participation in the political process. The majority of young people feel that party politics have little relevance to their lives, yet at the same time they are politically active in a broader sense. Many of the issues which young people regard as important cross the traditional lines of party politics and reflect concerns about global insecurity, injustice and environmental damage. Young people's engagement with politics can also be interpreted as reflecting a disintegration of older forms of collective identity as well as a scepticism about the extent to which meaningful processes of change are likely to emerge from within the traditional machinery of state.

Conclusion

In sum, this book aims to provide an assessment of conceptualizations of the new modernity through an empirical analysis of the social condition of youth in Britain. In doing so, a number of issues are raised which have important implications for sociological theory. Our central thesis is that while traditional sources of inequality continue to ensure the reproduction of advantage and disadvantage among the younger generation, various social changes have meant that these social cleavages have become obscure. Moreover, young people increasingly perceive themselves as living in a society characterized by risk and insecurity which they expect to have to negotiate on an individual level. While writers in the late modernist tradition, such as Beck (1992) and Giddens (1990, 1991), are able to illuminate some of these processes, we suggest that there has been a tendency to exaggerate changes and to understate many significant sources of continuity. In particular, it is argued that social class and gender remain central to an understanding of the lives of young people in the age of high modernity.

Notes

1 The terms 'late modernity' and 'high modernity' are used interchangeably.
2 Giddens uses the term 'ontological security' to refer to 'a sense of continuity and order in events' (1991: 243).
3 Recognizing the ways in which racial categories are socially structured and accepting the problems associated with using 'race' as an analytic concept, many writers place the word inside inverted commas (Miles 1982).

2 Change *and* continuity *in* education

In our view, Britain's education system is marked by low 'staying on'
rates and poor comparative performance because it is *divided*. Most
importantly, it divides 'academic' pupils from the rest through
different institutions, different curricula, different modes of study and
above all different qualifications which cater for the two groups.

(IPPR 1990)

Introduction

Many of the key characteristics of late modernity identified by Beck (1992)
and Giddens (1991) are reflected in changes within the British educational
system. Young people today face new risks at school which they are increasingly expected to negotiate as individuals rather than as members of a
collectivity. New forms of standardization have been introduced, alongside
different sources of diversification. The demand for advanced educational
credentials and flexible specializations associated with post-Fordist economies also means that individuals are constantly held accountable for their
performance and face increased risks should they fail. Collective identities
once manifest in class-based resistance to the school have weakened and
underlying class relationships have become obscure, although traditional
sources of inequality remain intact.

Many of the changes we describe are a direct consequence of educational policies introduced in the last two decades and some of the most
significant shifts have involved the construction of education as a consumer
product. Increasingly schools are having to sell themselves on the market
with parents being invited to select the 'product' best suited to the needs of
their child. While these changes facilitate individualized consumer choices,
the resources which social actors trade in the educational market place vary
considerably. People stand in differential positions in relation to the means
of consumption and have different amounts of 'cultural capital' (Bourdieu
1977) to trade in the educational market place. Consequently the rewards of
the educational system remain unequally distributed. The illusion of choice
created by the marketization of education masks the continued entrenchment
of traditional forms of inequality.

Although we argue that educational changes have had little impact
on patterns of social reproduction, new forms of educational provision and
an increased demand for an educated and trained labour force have had far
reaching effects on young people's experiences. In the Fordist era, the

availability of relatively unskilled positions in large manufacturing units meant that employment opportunities existed for minimum-aged, unqualified school-leavers. In cities across Britain in the 1950s and 1960s, young males made mass transitions from the classroom to the factories and building sites, while young women followed pathways leading straight from school to shops, offices and factories. As academic credentials were unnecessary for many working-class jobs, young people often had little incentive to strive for improved qualifications.

Prominent sociologists of the time frequently tried to explain differential performance and behaviour in schools in terms of the relative value of schooling for future careers (Ashton and Field 1976; Hall and Jefferson 1976; Willis 1977). Paul Willis (1977), for example, tried to account for the experiences of lower working-class boys in terms of their resistance to the middle-class culture of the school which was perceived as irrelevant to their futures as manual workers. In contrast to the ways in which working-class youth often rejected the middle-class definitions of success presented by their teachers, young people from privileged social backgrounds tended to develop an awareness that the maintenance of their economic and social advantages was partly dependent on their educational attainments. Their frames of reference, or what Bourdieu (1977) would refer to as their 'habitus', reinforced by experiences in the home and school, made these processes of social reproduction seem both natural and inevitable (Ashton and Field 1976; Brown 1987).

Strong patterns of differentiation in the educational system are a characteristic feature of industrial society. Until the late 1960s, the majority of working-class youths were educated after the age of eleven in separate institutions from their middle-class counterparts.[1] Even after the introduction of comprehensive schools, social class tended to affect the streams to which young people were allocated and the examinations for which they were entered (Ford 1969; Ball 1981). Young people from working-class families tended to move through the lower streams of the school while those from middle-class families tended to follow advantaged routes through the education system (Douglas 1967; Hargreaves 1967; Ball 1981).

In contrast, the post-industrial era has been characterized by a dramatic decline in the demand for unskilled youth labour and levels of post-compulsory educational participation have increased quite rapidly. In the modern labour market, employment contexts are increasingly differentiated and with increased competition for jobs, individual academic performance has become a prerequisite for economic survival (Beck 1992). In this context it has been argued that young people's relationships to the school have become individualized and that the class-based divisions which were once the key to understanding educational experiences have become diluted (Biggart and Furlong 1996). Caught in a situation where rejection of educational values or hostility towards school-based figures of authority almost guarantee long-term unemployment, class-based resistance becomes covert and young people are pitted against each other in a bid to maximize their educational attainments so as to survive in an increasingly hostile world. One of the consequences of these changes is that the lives of young people have become busier and more intense as they are increasingly forced to chase credentials which are often necessary to smooth the entry into the world of work (Büchner 1990).

These changes in young people's experiences of schooling have been seen as involving a dual process of standardization and diversification (Olk 1988, quoted in Chisholm *et al.* 1990). On the one hand, the majority of young people are spending a greater number of years in educational institutions and building up a range of qualifications which are regarded as helping them make an effective transition to the world of work. On the other hand, routes through the educational system have become more diverse as young people experience a greater range of academic and vocational courses which are often available within the same educational institutional setting (Heinz 1987; Chitty 1989). Yet while educational experiences have become more diverse, or individualized, class and gender have remained important determinants of educational pathways and attainments. Jones and Wallace, for example, have argued that 'paths to adulthood, far from being individualized, can still be predicted from social class origins to a great extent in both Britain and West Germany' (1990: 137). Indeed, Bourdieu (1977) predicted that the social and cultural advantages possessed by middle-class children would have a greater impact on levels of attainment as meritocratic educational policies became widespread, a theory which is supported by Zinneker (1990) who argues that 'cultural capital' has in fact become increasingly central to the reproduction of social advantage.

In this chapter we look at changing patterns of education in Britain and discuss the extent to which increasing levels of participation have been associated with a process of equalization. After reviewing the nature of these changes, we discuss some of the reasons why the diversification of experiences has had little impact on the strength of the relationship between social background and educational attainment. In this context, we argue that schools and other educational institutions in Britain remain divided with social class still representing a powerful determinant of 'success'; indeed, the 'universalism' envisaged by Beck (1992) would be hard to identify in the British educational system.[2]

Trends

Over the last two decades, education has come to play an increasingly prominent role in young people's lives. In 1972, the legal minimum school-leaving age was raised to 16, and the average length of schooling continued to rise among all social groups from this stage onwards. Moreover, some changes in the organization of education have helped to reduce the differences in educational experiences. The introduction of comprehensive schools, for example, has led to a broader social mix within institutions, while moves have also been made to teach young people with special needs within mainstream schools. These changes can each be seen as representative of a move towards a greater standardization of young people's experiences. Olk (1988, quoted in Chisholm *et al.* 1990) has linked this process of standardization to changes in the labour market and has argued that the greater demand for technical skills in the workplace has led to an increased demand for academic credentials and vocational training.

Changing patterns of participation

Changes in levels of educational participation have occurred both at the pre- and post-compulsory stages. Throughout the 1970s and 1980s there was a steady growth in the proportion of children under 5 years of age attending schools either on a full-time or part-time basis (CSO 1994), while at the post-compulsory stage changes have been much more far reaching. Minimum-aged school-leaving was once the predominant pattern, especially among young people from working-class families, but far fewer young people now leave school at 16 and most school-leavers continue to receive formal education or training on a part-time or block release basis (Furlong 1992; Roberts 1995; Surridge and Raffe 1995). Moreover, higher education, which was once the preserve of a small and privileged minority, has become part of the educational experiences of a growing number of young people (Smithers and Robinson 1989; Egerton and Halsey 1993).

Changing rates of post-compulsory educational participation between the 1970s and 1990s have been quite dramatic. In 1973/74, around a third of 16-year-old males (33 per cent) and less than four in ten females (37 per cent) participated in some form of full-time education in England. By 1993/94 more than seven in ten 16-year-olds (70 per cent of males and 76 per cent of females) participated in full-time education. Similarly, full-time participation among 17- and 18-year-olds more than doubled during this period (DES 1985; DFE 1994a) (Figure 2.1). While levels of participation in post-compulsory education have been increasing for over two decades, the most dramatic changes have occurred since the late 1980s. Between 1988 and 1993, for example, the proportion of 16-year-olds in full-time education increased by around 22 percentage points (DFE 1994a). Yet while observers had predicted a continued growth in post-16 participation rates (Raffe 1992), the latest figures show the first downturn in participation in over a decade (Spours 1995).

Although rates of participation in post-compulsory education have increased substantially, compared to many other developed countries levels of participation remain low and the educational system underfunded. In 1990, in Germany, France, Belgium, the USA, Denmark, Canada, the Netherlands and Japan, more than three-quarters of young people between the age of 16 and 18 remained in full-time education, compared to just 40 per cent in the UK (DFE 1993). However, if we take account of part-time study after the age of 16, rates of participation in Britain compare more favourably with more than 90 per cent of 16–18-year-olds participating in some form of full-time or part-time education in 1994/95 (Spours 1995). Yet the proportion of the British GNP spent on education still remains relatively low compared to other industrialized nations (CSO 1994). In terms of spending on education, Canada, for example, spends about 2.4 per cent of her GDP on tertiary

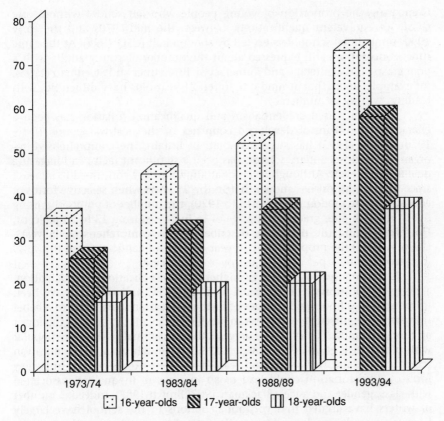

Figure 2.1   Participation in full time education (males and females)
Source: DES *Statistical Bulletin* (1985), DFE *Statistical Bulletin* (1994c)

education, while Britain spends just 0.1 per cent – substantially less than many countries in the former Eastern European bloc (the Czech Republic, Hungary and Poland spend about 1.6 per cent of GDP on tertiary education) (OECD 1995).

Qualifications

In Britain, changing patterns of schooling, together with the introduction of new forms of educational credentials and vocational courses, have had a significant impact on the qualification profiles of school-leavers. In 1970, a substantial proportion of young people left school without any graded examination result (44 per cent). Indeed, prior to 1972, many young people left school at the age of 15 without having sat any examinations. By 1991 unqualified school-leavers were in a small minority (6 per cent) (CSO 1994).

Comparing the proportion of young people who left school without any GCSEs or equivalent qualifications, between the mid-1970s and the early 1990s unqualified school-leavers fell by about a half (CSO 1994). At the same time, concerns are still expressed about the number of young adults with a poor grasp of basic literacy and numeracy skills. Bynner and Steedman (1995), for example, argue that around one in ten 21-year-olds have difficulties with reading, writing or numeracy.

While increased credentialism and qualification inflation has been a characteristic feature of developed countries in the post-war period (Dore 1976), Moon (1995) has suggested that, in Britain, the comprehensive re-organization of secondary schools has been a significant factor in increasing qualification levels. Although levels of attainment have continued to increase since the war, Moon has shown that in the 25 years when selective forms of education were predominant (1945 to 1970), the number of pupils obtaining five or more 'higher grades' at the age of 16 increased from 13 to 23 per cent. However, during the period he describes as the 'comprehensive 25 years' (1970 to 1995) the proportion of 16-year-olds with qualifications at this level increased from 23 per cent to just over 40 per cent.

In an attempt to encourage higher rates of educational participation, a range of vocational courses (such as TVEI, BTEC and GNVQ) have been introduced in schools and colleges of further education, partly due to a belief that the academic curriculum was somewhat irrelevant to those in the lower attainment bands. The evidence suggests that vocational options are popular with pupils (Bell *et al.* 1988; Lowden 1989), although vocational education tends to have a lower status and fears have been expressed that this new form of differentiation could lead to an increase in inequalities associated with class, gender and 'race' (Blackman 1987; Brown 1987). Indeed, a number of writers have argued that vocational options in the school have largely been taken up by working-class pupils in the lower attainment bands while leaving intact the traditional academic curriculum followed by middle-class pupils (Brown 1987; Chitty 1987).

Changes in the organization of education and the introduction of new forms of certification appear to have provided young people with greater incentives to remain at school (Raffe 1992); consequently they have had an impact on patterns of participation and achievement. Yet other socioeconomic changes have also had an impact on levels of attainment. Burnhill and colleagues (1990) have drawn attention to the relationship between the educational experiences of parents and children and have argued that an increasingly educated parentage has important implications for the educational outcomes of the new generation. However, Paterson and Raffe (1995) found that the association between parental education and rates of post-compulsory educational participation weakened over time and argued that more recent trends highlight a sharp rise in participation among young people whose parents had both left school at age 15. It is also important to recognize the ways in which changing patterns of employment and the demands of employers for a better educated labour force have affected educational attainments. Changing labour market structures have not simply provided positive incentives for young people to improve their qualifications;

the sharp decline in opportunities for minimum-aged school-leavers in many areas has produced an army of reluctant conscripts to post-compulsory education (see Chapter 3).

The continued expansion of qualified school-leavers together with raised quotas for admissions to higher education have also led to an increase in admissions to degree courses (Paterson 1992; Moon 1995; Smithers and Robinson 1995; Surridge and Raffe 1995). While throughout the industrialized world the numbers of young people entering higher education has been increasing since the Second World War, the changes which have taken place in Britain since the late 1980s have been particularly rapid. Moon (1995) has shown that between 1945 and 1970 the proportion of young people entering higher education rose from 6 per cent to 13 per cent; between 1970 and 1995 it increased to 39 per cent. Moreover, this rise has been particularly sharp over the last five years; the number of first year students on full-time courses in higher education in England increased by 91 per cent between 1982 and 1992, with an increase of 15 per cent between 1991 and 1992 (DFE 1994b). In Scotland, Surridge and Raffe (1995) have shown that the proportion of 19-year-olds in higher education increased from 16 to 31 per cent between 1987 and 1993.

Smithers and Robinson argue that 'six in ten of today's 18-year-olds can now expect to enter universities or colleges sooner or later in their lives' (1995: 1). Yet is important to note that this recent increase in student numbers has been disproportionately located in the 'new' universities (the former polytechnics) and that graduates of these institutions may face discrimination by employers. Indeed, it has been argued that the employment prospects of graduates have become increasingly stratified, with ex-students of the new universities facing the greatest difficulties in the labour market (Brown and Scase 1994). As Brown suggests, 'a degree from Oxford or an Ivy League University is judged to have a greater "capital" value than one from a little known college or university' (1995: 38). In this respect, an increase in university places is unlikely to be associated with an equalization of employment opportunities.

While more young people now experience higher education, legislative changes mean that they do so under increasingly difficult economic circumstances. In 1987 students were prevented from claiming supplementary benefit during short vacations, in 1990 they lost their entitlement to housing benefit and in the same year student loans were introduced and the value of the maintenance grant was frozen. In 1991 students lost their right to claim income support during the long vacation, and in 1993 the Chancellor, Kenneth Clarke, announced that cuts in student grants were to be implemented in subsequent years. In the face of a cut in funding allocations, universities are currently considering the introduction of top-up fees which would be paid by new students at the start of their courses. The Labour Party is proposing the introduction of a form of 'graduate tax' linked to national insurance contributions. Figures from the Department for Employment (1994) show that in 1970 just 8 per cent of students eligible for awards received less than half the full rate; by 1991 this had increased to 23 per cent. While parents contribute more, current estimates also show that the average student debt amounts to £1,982, with undergraduates expected to owe £3,021 by the end of their courses (*The Times*, 6 July 1996).

Commodification and choice

In many respects, the increasing range of courses which young people are able to follow is a reflection of changing political ideologies which have resulted in an increased tendency to treat education as a consumer product. Whereas social democratic governments tend to regard education as a means through which equality of opportunity can be increased, the Thatcher administration was committed to the introduction of free market principles involving greater choice for parents (Littlewood and Jönsson 1996).[3] The introduction of parental choice legislation in the 1980 Education Act for the first time gave parents the right to make a request to place their child in the school of their choice (subject to the availability of space). Parental choice legislation was supported by the introduction of a Parent's Charter in 1991 (amended in 1994) which provided information on the 'product' through making available details about school performance in the form of league tables, prospectuses, annual reports from the school governors, reports from school inspectors, and annual progress reports on pupils supported by testing at key stages. Other moves to strengthen the 'ideology of parentocracy' (Brown 1990) and increase choice included allowing schools to opt out of local authority control and permitting a degree of selectivity, the establishment of city technology colleges and an extension to the Assisted Places Scheme.[4] Describing trends in the new educational market place, Gewirtz suggests that 'schools (as producers) are now supposed to compete for the custom of children and their parents (as consumers)' (1996: 289), while the level of funding available to individual institutions is increasingly dependent on their success in the market place.

The implications of the commodification of education have been discussed in detail by educationalists (see for example Adler *et al.* 1989; Willms and Echols 1992; Ball *et al.* 1996). In the context of the current discussion, it is important to note that these changes are linked to the emergence of an epistemological fallacy: they help to create an illusion of equality while masking the persistence of old inequalities. By giving families greater responsibility for the type of education received by their children, negative outcomes can be attributed to poor choices on the part of the parents as customers. As a consequence, the state is able to relinquish some of its traditional responsibilities as the provider of an educational system based on social justice and underpinned by meritocratic principles. In a market orientated system,

> it is acceptable for there to be winners and losers, access to resources which is differentiated but unrelated to need, hierarchy, exclusivity, selectivity, and for producers to utilise whatever tactics they can get away with to increase their market share and to maximise profits. In short, there is pressure on individuals (both producers and consumers) to be motivated first and foremost by self interest.
>
> (Gewirtz 1996: 293)

In a study of the impact of parental choice in different local education authority areas, Ball and colleagues observed two key outcomes: 'First, choice is directly and powerfully related to social class differences. Second, choice emerges as a major factor in maintaining and indeed reinforcing social class divisions and inequalities' (1996: 110). Ball and colleagues (1996) predict that parental choice will reinforce social segregation as parents draw on their social and cultural advantages to select the best schools for their children. Other writers have argued that parental choice and the introduction of competition between schools leads to class and ethnic polarization (Adler *et al.* 1989; Willms and Echols 1992; Brown and Lauder 1996). Middle-class children, for example, are increasingly placed in schools with a 'name', while working-class children are left in schools with inferior resources which rapidly become ghettoized.

In sum, levels of educational participation have increased rapidly over the last two decades, but this expansion has not been matched by resources. Post-compulsory education has become a normal part of young people's experiences, even among those with relatively low attainments. Higher education, which was once the preserve of a small elite, has started to become a mass experience. While these changes can be seen as leading to a greater standardization of the experiences of young people in Britain, it is clear that there are parallel processes of diversification (Chitty 1989). Clear vocational and academic divisions are emerging within schools and the experience of higher education is becoming polarized between the old elite universities and the new universities with inferior resources and graduate employment rates (Brown and Scase 1994). Moreover, as a result of processes of commodification, schools are able to continue to reproduce social inequalities while maintaining a veneer of open access (Bourdieu and Passeron 1977). This process sustains the epistemological fallacy by helping to obscure the continued relevance of class to an understanding of differential outcomes in education.

Differentiated outcomes

As we move towards the establishment of a learning society where people face a continual need to develop their skills and credentials, it is important to reassess the extent to which old forms of inequality remain entrenched. Many of the reforms which have been implemented since the 1960s have explicitly aimed to boost the performance of low attaining groups, thereby reducing inequalities in educational attainment and helping to prevent a wastage of talent which can damage Britain economically. Other reforms have been introduced as a result of concern that the educational system was failing to deliver an adequate supply of suitably skilled personnel to meet the demands of employers operating in a technologically sophisticated global economy. Yet while it is true that some changes have had a measure of success, it has proved difficult to overcome the deeply embedded inequalities associated with class. On the other hand, gender differentiated patterns of attainment have become more equitable over the past two decades.

The persistence of class-based inequalities

Analyses of the effects of past periods of educational expansion have demonstrated that increasing levels of educational participation do not *necessarily* result in a process of equalization between social groups (Boudon 1973; Halsey *et al.* 1980; McPherson and Willms 1987). Using comparative data from several countries, Raftery and Hout (1990, quoted in Shavit and Blossfeld 1993) have suggested that educational inequalities associated with social class may remain entrenched until levels of middle-class participation approach 'saturation point'. Due to the expansion of tertiary education and the increase in the number of young people leaving school with recognized qualifications, the odds of a young person securing a place in higher education have increased dramatically. However, the evidence suggests that young people from working-class families remain less likely than their middle-class peers either to remain at school beyond the minimum leaving age, to leave school with a recognized qualification or to secure a place in higher education (Shavit and Blossfeld 1993).

The Department for Education and Employment does not routinely produce statistics on qualifications or staying-on rates which are broken down by social class, so in order to assess the extent to which changing patterns of participation have been associated with a more equitable distribution of qualifications it is necessary to use survey data. The Scottish Young People's Survey and the England and Wales Youth Cohort Study represent the most comprehensive sources of information on the effects of social background on educational attainment. These surveys both show that while participation in post-compulsory education has grown considerably among all social classes, strong differentials still exist. In Scotland in 1991, for example, 76 per cent of pupils with fathers in non-manual occupations began a first year of post-compulsory education compared to 41 per cent of those with fathers in manual occupations. A similar picture emerges in relation to higher education; 58 per cent of those from non-manual backgrounds entered higher education, compared to 20 per cent of those from manual backgrounds (Surridge and Raffe 1995).

Using data from the England and Wales Youth Cohort Studies, Payne (1995) showed that among the cohort who reached the age of 16 during the 1990/91 school year, staying-on rates varied from 84 per cent among young people with parents in professional, managerial and technical occupations to 51 per cent among those with parents working in semi- and unskilled and personal service occupations (Payne 1995). Moreover, she has argued that among the high-attainers, class-related differences in rates of post-compulsory participation narrowed considerably between 1989 and 1992.[5] However, over this same period there was an *increase* in class-based differentials among less qualified youth; comparing members of the highest and lowest socio-economic groups, differences in rates of participation increased by around 11 percentage points (Payne 1995).

Despite changes in levels of participation and the increasing number of qualified school-leavers found in all social classes, strong differences in levels of attainment persist. In Scotland in 1991, around four in ten young people

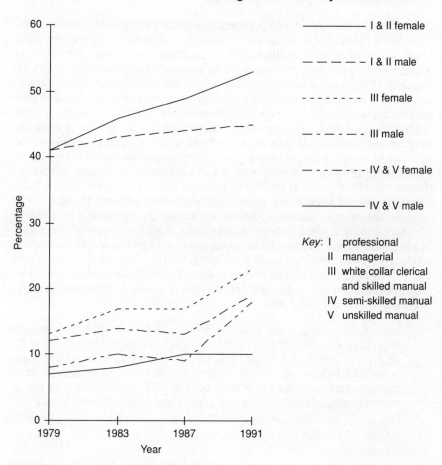

Figure 2.2 Young people in highest attainment band, by class and gender
Source: Scottish Young People's Surveys

from the lower working classes left school with minimal qualifications, compared to just over one in ten from the professional and managerial classes.[6]
Similarly almost half of the young people from the professional and managerial class achieved three or more Highers compared to less than one in five
of those with fathers in the lower working class. While there has been an
increase in the proportion of young people gaining three or more Highers,
class differentials remain strong (Figure 2.2).

Changing gender differentials

While educational inequalities associated with social class have remained
firmly entrenched, Figure 2.2 also illustrates the extent to which gender-
based inequalities in education have been transformed. Twenty years ago,

the underachievement of girls in the educational system was a major focus of sociological analysis. While girls tended to outperform boys in the early stages of primary school, their initial advantages were soon lost as boys began to overtake them in most areas of the curriculum (Douglas 1967). In the early 1970s, young women tended to gain fewer school-leaving qualifications and were underrepresented in the universities. Moreover, females who entered higher education frequently accepted places in colleges rather than universities and were overrepresented on vocational courses. Many explanations of the position of girls in the school made reference to differential patterns of socialization; it was argued that parents and teachers had lower expectations of females (which reflected disadvantages in the labour market) (Delamont 1980) and that girls faced pressure to limit their academic attainments for fear of frightening potential male suitors (Horner 1971).

By the early 1980s the situation had started to change and by the end of compulsory schooling girls were more likely than boys to possess a graded examination result, to have passed five or more O levels or one or more A levels (DES 1985). During the 1990s these gains have been consolidated and attention has turned to focus on the reasons for male underachievement in the education system. As Roberts argues, girls are now the educational high-flyers. By the mid-1990s, girls

> were maintaining their primary school lead over boys throughout secondary and into higher education. Girls today outperform boys in GCSEs, do better at A levels, and are more likely to enter higher education. Girls have also been making inroads into traditionally male subjects. They now do better than boys in GCSE maths and are a growing proportion of sixth form and higher education students in science and medicine. More young women than men are currently in medical schools training to be doctors.
>
> (1995: 47)

However, women are still underrepresented in certain subject areas (such as the sciences), are disadvantaged in the labour market and remain heavily concentrated in a few occupations which offer inferior rewards and prospects (see Chapter 3). The reasons for these changes in the relative performance of males and females are unclear. Changes in the labour market are likely to have had a powerful impact; females today grow up in a world where work has become much more central to the lives of women. These changes in work patterns are likely to have affected the educational expectations of parents and teachers and to have had an impact on patterns of gender socialization.

'Race' and inequality

Inequalities associated with 'race' also continue to be a cause for concern to educationalists with young people from certain ethnic minorities still tending to underperform at school in comparison to the white majority. In 1993, around a quarter of males and just less than a third of women of working age had no educational qualifications, while among the Pakistani and Bangladeshi community just over half of men and three-fifths of women lacked qualifications (CSO 1994). Using information from the England and Wales Youth Cohort Study, Drew and colleagues (1992) have shown that at the age of 16 the performance of white young people was around twice as high as that of Afro-Caribbeans, with the attainment of Asians being fairly close to the white majority. Some studies have also highlighted significant gender differences; Cross and colleagues (1990), for example, show that among Afro-Caribbeans, as among the white population, girls outperform boys.

While black youths still tend to underperform at school, it is important to be aware that 'colour' can often mask more significant forms of disadvantage. Among the black population, for example, unemployment rates tend to rise faster than among the white majority (Ohri and Faruqi 1988) while those who are employed are overrepresented in poorly paid occupations (Skellington and Morris 1992). In other words, the relatively poor attainment of young blacks perhaps has more to do with socioeconomic disadvantage than ethnicity. Indeed, Smith and Tomlinson (1989) have argued that within the secondary school, after controlling for attainment at age 11, there is little difference in the progress of black and white pupils. Once the post-compulsory stage of education is reached, Afro-Caribbeans and Asians (especially females) are more likely to remain in full-time education. In fact Drew and colleagues (1992) suggest that the parents of black youths are more likely to encourage their children to remain in education and that, *other things being equal*, the chances of Afro-Caribbeans experiencing post-compulsory education were three times higher than for whites while the chances of Asian youth remaining at school were ten times higher.

Spatial inequalities

The point, however, is that all things are not equal. Not only are black youths more likely to come from lower working-class families, they also tend to live in areas lacking in job opportunities and attend schools with poor records of attainment. Indeed, despite Giddens's (1991) claim that place has lost much of its significance, locality still constitutes an important dimension of structured inequality as many opportunities for social learning occur within small residential areas (Savage and Warde 1993). Using data from the Scottish Young People's Surveys, Garner and Raudenbush (1991) highlighted the significance of neighbourhood effects on young people's educational performance and argued that children from the most deprived home neighbourhoods performed less well than children with similar family backgrounds living in more advantaged home neighbourhoods. In an earlier study, Ashton and colleagues (1982) showed that after controlling for social class effects, young people living in St Albans were obtaining better qualifications than their counterparts in Sunderland. But geographical effects on educational attainment are not simply a function of patterns of neighbourhood deprivation. Over a long period of time, researchers have highlighted the negative impact of rural residence on educational attainment (Sewell *et al.* 1957; Sewell and Hauser 1993).

Inequalities in higher education

If we turn to consider the extent to which differential outcomes have been maintained in higher education, it is important to bear in mind that since 1945 the British system of higher education has been transformed from an elitist system catering for a small minority of young people to a system almost four in ten young people will experience at some time in their lives. This transformation of higher education has entailed increased recruitment among groups which were previously underrepresented, particularly young women and mature students, and has involved a shift from the old univer- sities to the former polytechnics (the new universities). Indeed, Smithers and Robinson argue that

> quadrupling the number of universities since 1960 and nearly doubl- ing it since 1990 has opened up university education to a much wider range of people . . . the universities are [now] somewhat less dominated by the sons and daughters of the professional and managerial classes.
>
> (1995: 4)

However, it is important not to overstate these changes in the social composition of higher education. The older universities still tend to be the preserve of children from professional and managerial backgrounds, while students in the new universities are more likely to come from working-class families with many entering as mature students or after having followed non- traditional academic pathways. In absolute terms, there has been a continuous growth in working-class participation, but relative changes have been minimal (Burnhill *et al.* 1990; Halsey 1992; Blackburn and Jarman 1993). Indeed, despite the far reaching changes which have occurred, class differentials in access to higher education have been maintained.

In an analysis of the changing relationship between social class and access to higher education, Egerton and Halsey (1993) compared the experi- ences of 25,000 people from three birth cohorts (those born between 1936 and 1945; between 1946 and 1955; and 1956 and 1965). The proportion of each social class who gained access to university before the age of 30 increased among each subsequent cohort, yet they argued that the process of change did not lead to an equalization of access. Between the first and the last birth cohort, the proportion of respondents from the service class who entered universities or polytechnics increased by 11.5 percentage points, the inter- mediate class increased access by 6.8 percentage points, while the representa- tion of the manual classes increased by just 2.9 percentage points. Similarly, in a study of inequalities in access to higher education between 1938 and 1990, Blackburn and Jarman argued that class inequalities showed little change and concluded by remarking that there was still 'a strong class differential among both men and women, and little has changed despite the large expansion of provision' (1993: 211). There are few comprehensive statistics on changing levels of participation among members of ethnic minorities. However, the available data suggests that most minority groups continue to be underrep- resented on degree courses (Skellington and Morris 1992).

While the social composition of universities and colleges has remained heavily skewed towards young people from relatively privileged social backgrounds, the biggest social change concerns the growing representation of young women in higher education. In the early 1960s, universities were still very male-dominated institutions and those females who did progress to higher education were disproportionately located in teacher training institutions. Crompton (1992) argues that until the 1970s any increase in educational participation of women tended to be absorbed in teacher training colleges. In 1965, 38,000 males and 15,000 females were admitted as undergraduates to British universities, yet admissions to teacher training colleges were skewed in the other direction: 26,000 females compared to 10,000 men (Crompton 1992). Throughout the 1970s and 1980s, female participation in higher education increased rapidly, partly reflecting their growing success within schools. By 1992, 47 per cent of full-time first year undergraduates were female. Indeed, Halsey (1992) shows that between 1970 and 1989 the number of males on full-time courses at the old universities rose by 20 per cent while female numbers increased by 114 per cent. In other words, while the recent expansion of higher education has helped to reduce gender inequalities, class-based barriers have proved more resilient.

Conclusion

Despite far reaching and radical changes in the British system of education its most characteristic feature has been retained: experiences which are highly differentiated. While the comprehensive reform of British schools provided a veneer of openness, it has been suggested that the maintenance of streaming and selection by neighbourhood effectively meant that differentiated forms of education survived (Ball 1981; Garner and Raudenbush 1991). While strong evidence is emerging to suggest that the academic performance of young people from working-class families has improved under a comprehensive system (McPherson and Willms 1987; Moon 1995), when put into perspective gains have been relatively small and wide differentials remain firmly entrenched. Although it is clear that meritocratic principles have been undermined by the barriers which stem from the ways in which education is organized in Britain, it is also true that, despite different modes of delivery, similar forms of inequalities exist across the industrialized world (Shavit and Blossfeld 1993). Indeed, Kerckhoff (1990) has suggested that although working-class Americans spend longer periods of time in full-time education than their British counterparts and while access to educational credentials is more equitable, patterns of social mobility in the two societies are very similar. In terms of the differentiation of outcomes, continuity rather than change best describes the British experience of education over the last two decades.

After having reviewed the evidence, it may be tempting to suggest that few significant changes have occurred and that therefore Beck was somewhat premature in his argument that post-industrial society is characterized by a growing individualism, yet we suggest that the evidence reviewed does in fact lend some support to his ideas. On an objective level, traditional structures of social inequality remain intact, but our perception of these processes has certainly been obscured by changes which have taken place. In Britain the process of individualization and the obscurity of traditional structures are highlighted by the outcomes of the Education Reform Act of 1988 which undermined the essential features of the comprehensive system. The collectivist principles which underpinned the comprehensive reforms of the late 1960s and early 1970s have been replaced by the process of marketization. As Gewirtz argues, 'concern for social justice is being replaced by a concern for institutional survival, collectivism with individualism, cooperation with suspicion, and need with expediency' (1996: 308). The continuing process of marketization (which is likely to be reinforced by a Labour Government committed to extending 'choice') mean that those who lack the cultural capital and information necessary to act as informed consumers will increasingly be marginalized as risks accumulate in such a way as to strengthen existing patterns of inequality while those with adequate resources can 'purchase safety and freedom from risk' (Beck 1992: 35).

Notes

1 Due to the highly localized catchments of primary schools, many young people spent their entire educational careers in the company of pupils who shared a similar social background.
2 Although the Scottish, English and Welsh educational systems are distinct in a number of ways, in our view the similarities are greater than the differences. In a European context, they are organized along similar lines and levels of post-compulsory participation are low.
3 Both Littlewood and Jönsson (1996) and Chitty (1989) show that despite an emphasis on free markets and decentralization, the Thatcher administration used a number of interventionist strategies which effectively reduced both local autonomy and the discretion of educationalists. The introduction of a national curriculum is an example of the centralization of decision making by a government committed to decentralization.
4 The Assisted Places Scheme aimed to provide places at fee paying schools for high-attaining pupils whose parents would not otherwise have been able to meet the full cost of private education.
5 High attainers are defined as those gaining five or more GCSEs at grades A–C.
6 The survey defined minimal qualifications as no passes at O grade or standard grade or passes at the lowest grades, which are sometimes regarded as 'fail' marks.

3 Social change *and* labour market transitions

In the past transitions were shorter and simpler ... By the 1980s
... there were no longer any clear, normal career patterns from which
most individuals could deviate. In this sense, individualisation had
become the norm.

(Roberts *et al.* 1994: 44)

Introduction

In the previous chapter we suggested that changing patterns of educational participation could partly be explained in terms of the restructuring
of the youth labour market. With a sharp decline in demand for unqualified,
minimum-aged, school-leavers, young people are remaining at school for
longer periods of time, partly due to the lack of opportunities to engage in
paid work. As a result of these changes, the transition from school to work
tends to take longer to complete and has become much more complex; this
has implications for domestic and housing transitions as well as for other life
experiences which will be discussed in later chapters.

The transition from school to work is often regarded as an important phase in the life cycle which holds the key to a greater understanding
of the ways in which social advantages and inequalities are passed from one
generation to the next. In the 1970s young people tended to make fairly direct transitions from school to full-time jobs; the situation in the mid-1990s
is very different. We suggest that short, stable and predictable transitions
are characteristic of a Fordist social structure in which the life experiences
of the masses are relatively standardized and homogenous. Over the last
three decades, transitions have changed in a number of ways. The transition
from school to work has become much more protracted (Roberts *et al.* 1987;
Roberts and Parsell 1992a), increasingly fragmented and in some respects less
predictable.

As Giddens suggests, social life in the modern world takes place in settings which are increasingly 'diverse and segmented' (1991: 83). Employment in manufacturing industry continues to decline, while the service sector
has become increasingly significant. For some commentators, these changes
represent a significant development in capitalist societies. Whereas the industrial revolution was accompanied by a sharp decline in agricultural employment, post-industrial society is characterized by a shrinking manufacturing

sector and the dominance of the service sector (Bell 1973). Alongside these changes, there has been a growth in part-time working and non-standard employment, employment in smaller work units, an increased demand for technical skills and 'flexible specializations' which together have been taken as characteristic of post-Fordist economies (Kumar 1995). In late modernity, individual skills and educational attainments are of crucial importance in smoothing labour market entry, while the collectivized transitions which were once central to an understanding of social reproduction have weakened.

For Beck (1992) these changes underpin the emergence of the risk society. Individuals are forced to assume greater responsibility for their experiences in the labour market and to constantly assess the implications of their actions and experiences. Life in the modern world involves a global insecurity of life (Jansen and Van der Veen 1992) and while successful labour market integration is achieved by some, others find themselves marginalized. Indeed, the increasing complexity of the skill market and the segmentation of labour means that young people can become vulnerable to long-term exclusion at an early stage in their lives.

In this chapter we describe the main changes in the youth labour market and in transitions from school to work and consider their implications for our understanding of processes of economic integration and the reproduction of inequalities based on class and gender. While there is strong evidence that school to work transitions have become more protracted, complex and differentiated, we are sceptical about the tendency to regard these changes as indicative of a new era in which social structures have become fragmented. However, we argue that structures have become more obscure as individuals have been made more accountable for their labour market fates. It is argued that two somewhat contradictory processes can be observed within modern societies: on the one hand a trend towards differentiation and diversity that reflects the economic transformations, which some interpret as leading to a post-industrial society, and on the other, the maintenance of stable, predictable transitions which help ensure that those occupying advantaged social positions retain the ability to transmit privileges to their offspring (Olk 1988, quoted in Chisholm *et al.* 1990). Finally, in the context of the risk society thesis, it is also important to examine the extent to which the greater protraction of transitions have led to growing unease and uncertainty as young people try to make sense of a world in which their future is perceived as risky and difficult to predict.

The changing youth labour market

Some of the key changes affecting the experiences of young people in Britain stem from the collapse of the youth labour market during the early 1980s and the restructuring of employment opportunities within a policy framework which placed priority on increased training, flexibility and securing a reduction in relative labour costs. With an increase in all-age unemployment caused by the economic recession, minimum-aged school-leavers increasingly faced difficulties securing work and by the mid-1980s, the majority of 16-year-old leavers were spending time on government sponsored training schemes (Furlong and Raffe 1989). These changes led to a fundamental restructuring of the youth labour market (Ashton et al. 1990) and had a radical impact on transitions from school to work. As a consequence, the number of young people leaving school to enter the labour market at age 16 declined sharply; in 1988, around 52 per cent of the school year cohort entered the labour market at the minimum age, compared to 42 per cent in 1990 and just 34 per cent in 1991 (Payne 1995).

The magnitude of these changes are highlighted through the evidence collected as part of the England and Wales Youth Cohort Study (YCS) and the Scottish Young People's Surveys (SYPS). Among the 1991 England and Wales cohort, less than one in five 16–17-year-olds (18 per cent) were in full-time employment more than six months after reaching the minimum school-leaving age (Courtenay and McAleese 1993), a decline of 9 percentage points since 1985.[1] Conducted biennially between 1977 and 1991, the SYPS can be used to provide information about changes in the destinations of young people over a longer period of time. By focusing on the declining group of young Scots who left school at the minimum age, the surveys show that in 1977, 72 per cent were in full-time jobs by the spring after leaving school; by 1991 this had declined to just 28 per cent.

In line with changes occurring throughout the industrialized world, the restructuring of the British economy has involved a continued decline in the manufacturing sector and the growth of employment in the service sector. Between 1970 and 1995, the total number of employees working in manufacturing industries fell from around 8.6 to around 3.8 million (Maguire 1991; DfEE 1996). During the 1980–83 recession, around a third of the jobs in the engineering industry were lost, a trend which affected the large number of young males who traditionally found employment in this sector (Maguire 1991). Over the same period, employment in the service sector increased from 11.3 to 16.2 million (Maguire 1991; DfEE 1996).[2] Whereas school-leavers in many industrial centres once made mass transitions from school to manufacturing employment, today they tend to work in smaller scale service environments and are less likely to be working with large numbers of other young people or sharing work experiences with their peers. By 1991, nearly half of the 18–19 age group were working in firms with less than 24 employees. Yet school-leavers with the highest qualifications tend to work in large firms, while the least qualified tend to be concentrated in small firms (Park 1994).[3] In this respect the work situations of low-attaining youth have become more individualized.

Associated with these changing employment contexts, there has been a weakening of collectivist traditions manifest in the decline of the trade unions which has been reinforced by legislation to curb their powers. Between 1979 and 1993 the number of trade unions fell from 453 to 254 (DfEE 1995), and membership fell equally dramatically. In 1977, around half of the workforce were members of trade unions; by 1994 this had declined to around 30 per cent. Moreover, rates of union membership tend to be lowest in the growing sectors of the economy in which young people are heavily represented (sales and personal and protective services) (Maguire 1991; DfEE 1996). In the hotel and restaurant sector and in sales, for example, only around one in ten employees are members of trade unions, while among professionals around one in two are members (CSO 1996).

As trade unions once provided young people with an introduction to working-class politics and collective action, the decline in union membership has implications for political socialization (see Chapter 8). While there have been few studies of young people and trade unions, Spilsbury and colleagues (1987) argue that levels of unionization among young people are primarily determined by overall patterns of union activity within an industry or firm. As a result of recent industrial changes, young people are increasingly finding employment in small firms and in areas where union activity has traditionally been weak. However, in a study of firms in the Swindon area, Rose noted that even in manufacturing industries, young employees displayed a 'sheer lack of interest' in trade unions (1996: 126).

One particularly significant change in the youth labour market is that which stems from the development of 'flexible' employment practices. The recession of the 1980s provided employers with an incentive to seek ways of reducing labour costs and one of the ways in which this was achieved was through the increased use of part-time and temporary workers (Ashton *et al.* 1990).[4] Indeed, during the 1980s, many firms reduced their core workforces and created a periphery of workers, many of whom were females working part-time hours or provided through government funded schemes (strategies which relieved employers of a number of financial obligations, such as the provision of sick pay or the payment of national insurance contributions) (Atkinson 1984). The concentration of women in certain sectors of the labour market has led to the argument that women's labour market prospects are restricted both by horizontal segregation (by occupation) and vertical segregation (with upward mobility chances being restricted in all occupational sectors) (Hakim 1979).

In this context it is important to note that young service workers tend to be concentrated in the lower tier services (Krahn and Lowe 1993), frequently have little control over their working environment and often have poor job security. Among 18–19-year-olds in 1991, nearly eight in ten young women (76 per cent) and nearly three in ten young men (28 per cent) worked in lower tier services such as clerical, personal service and sales work (Park 1994). The poor working conditions of young service workers have been highlighted in the British press where attention was drawn to part-time employees at Burger King who were apparently forced to clock out at those times during the day when customer demand was low. Krahn and Lowe (1993) report that Burger King in Toronto restricts shifts to three hours so as to avoid having to provide workers with breaks.

With a shortage of job opportunities for young people, some survive through marginal employment, described by MacDonald (1996) as 'fiddly jobs'. According to MacDonald, young people become engaged in the marginal economy as a survival strategy, and they take up 'fiddly jobs' because of the shortage of mainstream job opportunities and because of the difficulties in surviving economically on benefits (MacDonald 1996). Although self-employment among young people has risen, most of those who become self-employed have few academic qualifications and their businesses have a high failure rate (Park 1994; MacDonald 1996).[5]

Unemployment and schemes

For young people, unemployment and the threat of unemployment has had a strong impact on recent labour market experiences. As Mizen (1995: 2) argues,

> today, in the 1990s, far from being easy, finding a job directly from school has been the exception rather than the rule and many young workers are now forced to confront realities of a hostile labour market in a way unimaginable even 20 years ago.

Youth unemployment increased fairly steadily from the late 1970s to the mid-1980s, declined over a period of about three years and then from 1989 began to increase again. Unemployment among the 16–17 age group increased from 9 per cent among males and females in 1977, to 13 per cent of males and 14 per cent of females in 1993 (OPCS 1995). Among the 18–24 age group unemployment increased from 7 per cent of males and 6 per cent of females in 1977, to 18 per cent of males and 11 per cent of females in 1993 (Figure 3.1).

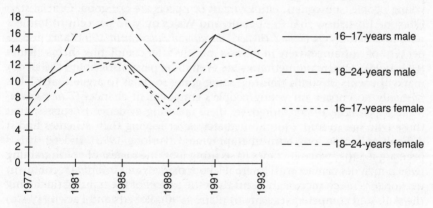

Figure 3.1   Proportion of age group unemployed
Source: OPCS 1995

   For young people leaving school at age 16 and 17, the introduction of government training schemes must be regarded as one of the most significant changes affecting transitional patterns. From the mid-1970s, as levels of youth unemployment increased, youth training schemes were introduced. The first scheme specifically aimed at young people (the Job Creation Programme) was introduced in 1975 in order to provide temporary work experience for school-leavers without jobs. At this stage, a small minority of young people experienced schemes, but with the introduction of the Youth Opportunities

Programme (YOP) in 1978 providing six months of work experience for those who had been unemployed for six weeks, levels of participation grew. In 1981, YOP was succeeded by the year-long Youth Training Scheme (YTS) and in 1986 YTS became a two-year programme (subsequently renamed YT and, more recently, Skillseekers).

By the mid-1980s, with a majority of minimum-aged school-leavers having had experience of YTS (Furlong and Raffe 1989), schemes had become central to an understanding of the transition from school to work. In 1985, 20 per cent of males and 14 per cent of females in England and Wales were on YTS in the spring after reaching the minimum school-leaving age (Courtenay 1988). By 1989, participation had increased to account for the spring destinations of 27 per cent of males and 20 per cent of females, but thereafter started to decline (as educational participation grew). In spring 1992, 16 per cent of males and 13 per cent of females were on YT (Courtenay and McAleese 1993). With the collapse of the youth labour market and the subsequent withdrawal of social security and unemployment benefit, today's 16-year-olds tend to face a choice between remaining in full-time education or finding a place on a scheme. In some areas the range of training opportunities has been limited; young people have been sceptical about the value of the programmes and hostile towards the low allowance provided (Raffe· and Smith 1987; Raffe 1989).

Despite government claims that YT has helped increase the skill level of young people, subsequent employment prospects are not good. Official statistics for 1994 show that in England and Wales only 42 per cent of trainees were awarded NVQs (*Times Higher Educational Supplement* 1994) and just 56 per cent of ex-trainees were in jobs six months after completing their schemes (DEE 1995).[6] Other commentators are even more pessimistic about the labour market benefits of youth training; some going so far as to argue that YT has 'virtually no impact' on young people's employment chances (*Times Educational Supplement* 1989). Moreover, there is strong evidence to suggest that those who fail to find a job immediately after leaving their schemes find it difficult to escape long-term unemployment (Furlong 1993). Indeed, it has been argued that when it comes to securing jobs, the *context* of youth training (which includes contact with internal labour markets and informal recruitment networks) is much more significant than the *content* of the training (including the skills and competencies gained) (Raffe 1990). Roberts and Parsell (1992b) also argue that the stratification of youth training results in a diversity of experiences with some young people (primarily working-class trainees with few qualifications and members of ethnic minorities) being trained in contexts where the chances of employment are virtually nil.

Although the government has tried to make political mileage out of the claim that it has helped raise training standards among young people, there is clear evidence to show a continued decline in apprentice training stretching back to the mid-1960s. In 1964, there were 235,000 male apprentices and 5,400 female apprentices in manufacturing industries. By 1989 this had declined to 49,700 and 3,900 respectively (Layard *et al.* 1994). Moreover, these figures do not simply reflect the general decline in manufacturing. As a proportion of all employees in manufacturing, apprentices fell from 3 per cent to 1 per cent over the same period (Layard *et al.* 1994). Despite the rapid growth of the service sector, the number of apprentices in all industries has declined in recent years (from 332,000 in 1984 to 191,000 in 1995) (CSO 1996; Deakin 1996).

Discouraged workers

While government investment in training schemes has been justified by the need to increase skill levels in order to provide a labour force which can compete in a global economy, Ashton and colleagues have argued that the measures introduced by governments during the 1980s actually produced a 'mismatch between the supply flow of young people entering the labour market and the demands of employers for a highly educated labour force' (1990: 2). Effectively, government intervention during this period strengthened a national system of training geared towards 16- and 17-year-old school-leavers which discouraged continued educational participation. Ironically, increases in educational participation, which have the potential to deliver highly quali-fied workers, occurred primarily through a lack of consumer confidence in the product (YT) being offered by the government.

In the previous chapter we highlighted the rapid growth in the num-bers of young people remaining in full-time education beyond the age of 16, a trend which has been stimulated by changes occurring in the youth labour market since the 1980s. With a rapid decline in the number of jobs avail-able to minimum-aged school-leavers and the growth of a 'surrogate labour market' (Lee *et al.* 1990) involving the introduction and development of various youth training schemes, remaining in full-time education has provided young people with a credible alternative and has been perceived by some as involving less risk than direct entry into a contracting labour market. Recent work in Scotland, England and Wales has highlighted this relationship be-tween labour markets and post-compulsory educational participation. Using Scottish data, Raffe and Willms (1989) argued that in labour markets with above average rates of unemployment, fewer young people leave school at the minimum age, the effect being strongest among those with mid-range qualifications who may have been on the margins of deciding whether to leave or stay. However, in an attempt to replicate the Scottish analysis using data from England and Wales, Gray and colleagues (1992) failed to find a comparable 'discouraged worker' effect; indeed, they found that in England more young people stayed on at school in low unemployment areas. In a subsequent analysis, Paterson and Raffe (1995) reconsidered their earlier con-clusions. In this new analysis, they concluded that the 'discouraged worker' effect seemed to be weaker among more recent cohorts of young people and they explained this change in terms of a general weakening of the pull from the labour market on young people as job opportunities continued to decline for all young people.

In sum, the significant changes which have occurred in the youth labour market during the 1980s and early 1990s provide some support for the idea that Britain is becoming a post-industrial society. Young people are increasingly finding work in the service sector while skill development and 'flexible specialization' have become necessary for young workers in the struggle to avoid long-term unemployment and economic and social marginalization. These changes can be seen as arising from economic rather than political processes (Green 1989; Ashton *et al.* 1990). While Thatcherite policies helped strip away legislative frameworks developed in the Fordist era, the main changes in the youth labour market were undoubtedly caused by changes in the global economy following the recession of the early 1980s (Green 1989; Ashton *et al.* 1990). The decline in union power, for example, was accelerated by legislation and confrontation, yet the root cause was to be found in the decline of employment in large scale industrial units and the growth of the small private firms.

The diversification of labour market transitions and the maintenance of structured inequalities

Changes occurring over the last decade appear to have radically altered the nature of young people's labour market participation. Transitions to employment now tend to take longer to complete, while the diversification of routes means that experiences have become more individualized. Indeed, many researchers have highlighted the increasing complexity of the transition from school to work with young people finishing school at different stages and following a variety of overlapping routes into the labour market (Clough *et al.* 1986; Furlong and Raffe, 1989). Between the ages of 16 and 18, young people build up a far greater range of experiences than previously; they embark on different courses of study, receive training in a number of contexts, and spend time both out of work and in employment. From the stage that they leave school until they obtain their first full-time jobs, few young people share identical sets of experiences and most encounter situations where they are able to select between competing sets of alternatives (Roberts 1995). In this context Roberts suggests that a process of individualization has occurred in so far as these changes have involved a reduction in the number of young people with closely matching transitional patterns.

Differentiated experiences

However, the existence of individualized or diversified routes should not be taken as an indication that structural determinants of transitional outcomes have weakened. On a number of different levels, young people's transitional experiences can be seen as differentiated along the lines of class and gender. Indeed, we suggest that in many crucial respects, continuity rather than change best describes the trends of the last two decades.

Despite an apparent increase in the possibilities to continue full-time education or embark on a course of training, young people from advantaged positions in the socioeconomic hierarchy have been relatively successful in protecting privileged access to the most desirable routes. Although young people from working-class families are increasingly likely to remain at school beyond the age of 16, they continue to be overrepresented among early labour market entrants; in 1992 around 6 per cent of the children of professional workers were in full-time jobs at the age of 16–17 compared to more than one in five of those from the manual classes (Courtenay and McAleese 1993). Moreover, there is no evidence to suggest that class-based differentials have declined over the last decade (Hoskins *et al.* 1989; Furlong 1992; Marshall and Swift 1993), although those from ethnic minorities are becoming more likely than their white counterparts to avoid early labour market entry (Courtenay and McAleese 1993).

The timing of entry to full-time jobs has also continued to be strongly affected by gender: while girls tend to stay on at school, boys are more likely to have entered full-time jobs by the age of 16–17. Of those reaching the minimum leaving-age in 1991, for example, 22 per cent of boys but just 14 per cent of girls were in full-time jobs by the following spring (Courtenay and McAleese 1993). This differential has increased since the mid-1980s, reflecting an increased tendency for young women to remain in full-time education which is partly explained by the demands of service sector employers for educated female workers. The increased demand for female service workers has also been reflected in narrowing wage differentials. At age 18–19 women still tend to earn less than men (92 per cent of the male wage in 1991), yet they work fewer hours and once these differences have been taken into account, the difference between male and female workers is in the order of 2 per cent (Park 1994). However, there is evidence to suggest that wage inequalities increase with age (Martin and Roberts 1984; Dex 1985).

Similarly, experiences of youth training have remained highly stratified by class, gender and 'race'. Those from working-class families have always been more likely than middle-class youths to join training schemes (Furlong 1992; Roberts and Parsell 1992b; Courtenay and McAleese 1993), and quality training tends to be reserved for those with strong academic credentials (who are often from the more advantaged class positions). A number of writers have noted the ways in which the most disadvantaged young people and those from ethnic minorities tend to be concentrated in certain schemes with low rates of post-training employment (Lee *et al.* 1990; Roberts and Parsell 1992b). These second-rate training schemes have been variously described as 'sink schemes' or the 'warehousing' schemes (Roberts and Parsell 1992b). It has also been argued that schemes serve to reinforce gender stereotypes in the labour market (Cockburn 1987) and that scheme employers often lack an awareness of equal opportunities issues (Lee *et al.* 1990).

While levels of unemployment have increased in a general sense, again most young people who spend significant periods of time out of work come from working-class families and are located in parts of Britain which have been badly hit by recession and by the restructuring of labour markets (Ashton *et al.* 1982; Roberts *et al.* 1987; Furlong and Raffe 1989; White and McRae 1989). Among those who reached the minimum school-leaving age in 1991, just 2 per cent of those with parents in professional occupations were unemployed the following spring, compared with around one in ten of those with parents in manual occupations (Courtenay and McAleese 1993). Moreover, while 7 per cent of white respondents were unemployed at this stage, 12 per cent of black respondents, 8 per cent of Asians and 14 per cent of those from other ethnic groups reported themselves as unemployed (Courtenay and McAleese 1993). Differences in levels of unemployment among various ethnic groups are even more significant among older age groups. Between the ages of 16 and 24, unemployment is significantly higher among Afro-Caribbeans (40 per cent), Pakistanis and Bangladeshis (35 per cent) while the unemployment rate among the Indian population is similar to that of the white population (20 per cent) (DfEE 1994).

Although all young people have become increasingly vulnerable to unemployment, in recent years there has been a disproportionate increase in male unemployment which has been observed in a number of European countries (Hammer 1996). Whereas in the late 1970s unemployment rates among the 18 to 24 age group were similar for both sexes, by 1993 the male unemployment rate was 4 percentage points above the female rate. Among graduates, the unemployment rate is also higher among males; a year after graduation, 12 per cent of males are unemployed, compared to 8 per cent of women (*Sunday Times* 1995). Males are also likely to be unemployed for longer periods of time than females; in 1995, around 127,000 males in the 18 to 24 age group had been unemployed for a year or more, compared to 38,000 women (*Sunday Times* 1995). These differences are partly explained by the decline in the manufacturing sector (traditionally an important source of employment for males) and the growth of the service sector (in which many jobs traditionally performed by females have been located). Yet differential patterns of labour market withdrawal among the unemployed are also significant.

Of those who experience unemployment after completing education or training, some young people subsequently withdraw from the labour market. Most of those who withdraw have substantial experience of unemployment, with young women being twice as likely to withdraw than males (Furlong 1992). Once a young person gives up hope of finding a job, labour market withdrawal may represent an option which provides positive psychological benefits. Indeed, for young women, especially those who are married or have children, withdrawal may be a socially acceptable alternative to long-term unemployment.

Reconceptualizing transitions

The changes in the youth labour market described in this chapter have been reflected in the different ways in which sociologists have conceptualized the transition from school to work. In the 1960s and 1970s, the predictability of transitional routes tended to be stressed (Carter 1962; Roberts 1968; Ashton and Field 1976; Willis 1977). Within these models, social class and gender were seen as powerful predictors of school experiences and educational attainment, which in turn helped determine the nature of the transition and the positions young people entered in the labour market. Ashton and Field (1976), for example, identified three main routes which young people followed from school to work: 'extended careers' involving higher education and access to the graduate labour market; 'short-term careers' involving short periods of training or post-compulsory education and leading to skilled manual or routine white collar employment; and 'careerless' routes which involved leaving school at the minimum age to take up semi-skilled or unskilled employment. With young people being allocated to distinct routes at an early age, this model corresponds to the train journey metaphor described earlier. In a context of collectivized transitions, young people were provided with clear messages about their destinations and the likely timing of their journeys and tended to develop an awareness of likely sequences of events.

With the transition from school to work tending to become much more complex during the 1980s, it became increasingly difficult for minimum-aged school-leavers to secure jobs immediately after leaving school and routes into work tended to become more diverse. Yet despite this diversification of routes, sociologists tended to argue that transitional outcomes remained highly structured (Roberts *et al.* 1987; Bynner and Roberts 1991; Banks *et al.* 1992). This structural emphasis was underlined by the use of the term 'trajectory', implying that individuals had little control over their destinations (Evans and Furlong 1997).

Reflecting the theoretical influence of Beck and Giddens, transitional models introduced during the 1990s have tended to place a greater emphasis on the ways individuals actively negotiate risk and uncertainty, referred to by Evans and Furlong (1997) as a 'navigation' model and loosely corresponding to the analogy of a switch from rail transport to road travel (see Chapter 1, this volume). In the age of high modernity, the range of possibilities open to individuals means that people are constantly forced to engage with the likely consequences of their actions on a subjective level. Indeed, Beck highlights the extent to which 'reflexive modernization' involves an ongoing 'self-confrontation with the effects of risk' (1994: 5).

The emphasis placed on subjective perceptions of risk and uncertainty represents an important break with earlier traditions. Prior to the 1990s, the predominant theme was that having followed well-trodden and predictable routes or trajectories from the family, through the school and into the labour market, the transition from school to work tended not to be associated with a subjective unease or discomfort (Carter 1962; Ashton and Field 1976). Although we remain sceptical about the extent to which changes in the youth labour market have affected underlying patterns of social reproduction, we recognize that processes which appear stable and predictable on an objective level may involve greater subjective risk and uncertainty.

During the 1960s and 1970s, as a consequence of following highly structured trajectories from school into the labour market, young people tended to develop sets of assumptions which helped make their experiences seem natural and normal. After spending their formative years in socially restricted networks, young people usually developed an awareness of the range of opportunities likely to be available to people like themselves and the nature of the associated lifestyles. Consequently Ashton and Field (1976) maintained that the transition from school to work, generally being a confirmation of earlier experiences and expectations, was a smooth and relatively untraumatic event in the lives of most young people.

In many ways, processes of social reproduction which are smooth and predictable on a subjective level can be regarded as characteristic of a traditional social order in which children, following in the footsteps of their parents, may not give very much consideration to a wider range of jobs or careers. In communities with a limited range of job opportunities young people may tailor their expectations to the main types of jobs available. In the mining communities of the Northeast and in the Welsh valleys, boys often grew up expecting to follow their fathers down the pits (Dennis *et al.* 1956). In the West Midlands, Willis (1977) highlighted subjective continuities among working-class males who celebrated the masculine culture represented on building sites and the factory floor. The strength of these assumptions in traditional working-class communities is also emphasized by Carter (1962) who found a widespread expectation that boys would enter the steel trade. Similar patterns have been identified among females. Westwood (1984), for example, argued that working-class girls expected to enter the textile factories of the East Midlands before withdrawing to become involved in full-time domestic labour.

The restructuring of the adult labour market and the decline of the youth labour market have important implications for the way young people experience the transition to work on a subjective level. These changes, which stem from the continued decline in demand for low skill labour, have led to a demand for a better educated, more skilled labour force in advanced industrial societies. But the speed of change has meant that the current generation of young people are making their transitions to work in a period of turmoil and, as a consequence, may lack the clear frames of reference which can help smooth transitions. In this respect, entry to the world of work in the 1990s is characterized by a heightened sense of risk.

Having parents who experienced very different transitions, young people often perceive the process as filled with risk and uncertainty. Many, fearing the consequences, shelter from the labour market as long as possible by remaining in education (Biggart and Furlong 1996). Yet it is important to stress that subjective perceptions of risk can be present even among those whose routes appear relatively safe to the outside observer; even young people from privileged social backgrounds and with excellent academic credentials frequently worry about failure and about the uncertainty surrounding future events and experiences (Lucey 1996).

Conclusion

In this chapter we have highlighted the extent to which labour market experiences of young people have changed over the last two decades. The types of jobs which young people enter and their experiences of the transition from school to work have changed quite significantly, largely as a result of global economic changes in the demand for labour. Although greater opportunities for advanced education and training are available to all young people, existing social disadvantages seem to have been maintained. Indeed, young people from working-class families and ethnic minorities face a new set of disadvantages which stem from the development of a labour market periphery. New forms of flexible working have reduced job security and many of the least qualified young people have become trapped on the labour market periphery and are vulnerable to periodic unemployment. Moreover, the creation of opportunities in small service environments has been associated with a decline in collective traditions and union membership for working-class youth, while the professional and technical middle classes have become more organized and increasingly unionized (Lash and Urry 1987). In this respect, we agree with Jessop and colleagues who argue that post-Fordism is characterized by a 'division between a skill-flexible core and a time-flexible periphery, which is now replacing the old manual/non-manual division' (1987: 109).

While the demand for flexible, skilled workers in the new information society creates advantages for some young people, the continued segmentation of labour markets helps ensure that traditional privileges are protected. Yet despite the maintenance of traditional lines of inequality, subjectively young people are forced to reflexively negotiate a complex set of routes into the labour market and in doing so, develop a sense that they alone are responsible for their labour market outcomes. It is in this context that we suggest that a transitional metaphor based around car journeys reflects the pattern of change. Young people are forced to negotiate a complex maze of potential routes and tend to perceive outcomes as dependent upon their individual skills, even when the objective risks of failure are slim. In turn, the perception of risk can lead to subjective discomfort. The evidence we have presented in this chapter provides some support for Beck and Giddens. Transitions have become more individualized and young people from all social backgrounds perceive their situations as filled with risk and uncertainty. At the same time, there is also evidence that, on an objective level, risks are distributed in an unequal fashion and correspond closely to traditional lines of disadvantage based on class and gender.

Notes

1 Courtenay and McAleese (1993) argue that the process of self-classification tends to lead to an overestimate of full-time employment while underestimating scheme participation. They suggest that the proportion in full-time employment could be nearer 15 per cent.

2 In 1991 37 per cent of 18–19-year-old males and 6 per cent of females worked in manufacturing industries (Park 1994).

3 In 1991 more than eight in ten young people with A levels worked in firms with over 24 employees, while over a third of those with no GCSE qualifications were employed in firms with less than nine employees.

4 In 1991, around a third of 18–19-year-olds reported having had a part-time job since the age of 16 (Park 1994).

5 Among 18–19-year-olds in 1991, 4 per cent of male and 1 per cent of females were self-employed.

6 A number of training initiatives have been introduced with the aim of developing skills among young people. Two of these are of particular significance: Training Credits, which will be received by all 16–17-year-olds leaving full-time education in 1996 and which can be used to 'buy' suitable training; and Modern Apprenticeships which have been introduced with the aim of increasing the number of young people receiving craft and technical training up to NVQ level 3. At this stage it is not possible to provide a full evaluation of either of these initiatives.

4 Changing patterns *of* dependency

> The outcome of policies privatizing the welfare of young people onto
> their families by extending parental responsibilities is that family
> support is now a crucial factor in determining young people's life
> chances, and those without it are at greatest risk. Yet, for a variety
> of reasons, access to family support may have become more difficult.
>
> (Jones 1995: 12)

Introduction

The changing patterns of schooling and the protraction of the school to
work transition which have been discussed in the previous two chapters
have led to an extension in the period during which young people remain
dependent on the family and the state. As financial independence through
employment provides young people with the resources to leave the parental
home and establish more autonomous patterns of residence, extended school
to work transitions will have an impact on patterns of dependency. Yet in
modern Britain adult status tends not to be conferred solely on the basis of
successful completion of the school to work transition, but can be linked to
the completion of a series of linked transitions. Coles (1995) suggests that
there are three interrelated transitions made by young people, some of which
must be achieved before being accepted into adult society. Aside from the
transition from school to work, young people may make a domestic transition,
involving a move from the family of origin to the family of destination, and
a housing transition involving a move to residence away from the parental
(or surrogate parental) home. These three transitions are interrelated in so far
as experiences in one dimension of life will have an impact on other life
events; a school to work transition which is interrupted by unemployment,
for example, is likely to affect the stage at which young people make domestic
and housing transitions.

The extension of transitions, together with changes in typical sequences
of events, has implications for the establishment of identity and for processes of individualization and risk. While it can be argued that over the last
two decades all three transitions have become more complex and difficult to
complete (Coles 1995), our interest in this chapter is to explore the implications of the extension of youth dependency for the construction of identity
and to assess the extent to which new patterns of individualization and risk
can be linked to changes in domestic and housing transitions. We argue that
recent social changes, which have led to an enforced increase in the period of

youth dependency, have resulted in a situation in which the future is often seen as filled with risk and uncertainty; in such circumstances it can be difficult to maintain a stable identity. Changes in family structures, together with the introduction of recent social policies, represent a new set of hazards to be negotiated by today's youth and those with access to the appropriate social and economic resources remain less vulnerable to the consequences of failure. In this context we suggest that the ability to make successful transitions to adulthood are still powerfully conditioned by 'traditional' inequalities such as class and gender.

The extension of semi-dependency

In the modern world, youth is an intermediate stage in the life cycle. In law, children are regarded as dependent and in need of protection while adults are regarded as full citizens and expected to take responsibility for their own lives (Coles 1995). Young people are treated differently from children, granted certain rights and responsibilities, but denied the full range of entitlements accorded to adults (Jones and Wallace 1992; Coles 1995). Full citizenship is not automatically conferred on reaching a certain age and, as Coles suggests, 'there is no clear end to the status of childhood and no clear age at which young people are given full adult rights and responsibilities' (1995: 7). Moreover, the legal rights and responsibilities which signify adulthood are granted in stages, some of which are based on chronological age, others being dependent on the completion of stages in the transitional process (such as the completion of full-time education). Young people are able to engage in some part-time employment at the age of 13, can leave school and enter full-time employment at 16 but cannot marry without parental consent or vote in elections until 18 and are not entitled to full 'adult' social security benefits until the age of 25 (Harris 1990; Craig 1991; Coles 1995). Youth is therefore a period of social semi-dependency which forms a bridge between the total dependence of childhood and the independence of adulthood. Consequently it is largely defined in the negative – by what it is not, rather than by what it is. A youth is no longer a child, but is not quite a mature adult living an independent life. As a stage in the life cycle which lacks clearly defined boundaries, the period we refer to as youth is historically and socially variable. Just as childhood became recognized as a distinct part of the life course during a specific period of industrial development (Aries 1962), the terms 'youth' and 'adolescence' are social constructs which emerged at a particular stage of socioeconomic development.

The term adolescence was first used by Stanley Hall (1904) to describe a physiological process linked to the onset of puberty and sexuality in young people, with psychologists tending to regard adolescence as a period of physical, sexual and emotional development occurring between the ages of about 12 and 18. However, the onset of puberty, being affected by nutritional standards, occurs earlier now than in the past (Donovan 1990). Psychologists also developed an interest in the ways in which individuals came to terms with these physiological changes and established adult identities (e.g. Erikson 1968). Since the 1920s, psychologists have tended to make a distinction between the physiological process of maturation and the social processes through which young people come to terms with their new statuses and develop adult identities. Bühler (1921, quoted in Coleman and Husen 1985), for example, referred to the process of social and psychological maturation as *Kulturpubertät* or 'cultural puberty'. Despite this refinement in psychological approaches, it is important to make the distinction between the term 'adolescence', which still tends to be used primarily in a psychological context, and 'youth' which has traditionally been the focus of sociological investigations. Whereas adolescence is seen as covering a limited time span, the term youth covers a much broader period of time; extending today from the mid-teens to the mid-twenties (Springhall 1986). Unlike adolescence, youth is a social concept which lacks a physiological base.

Being defined as a period of semi-dependency which young people pass through prior to the granting of adult status, youth is historically and socially variable because the attainment of independent adulthood is conditioned by social norms, economic circumstances and social policies. Illustrating the historical variability of the life stage referred to as youth, Springhall (1986) argues that in the early modern period, young people frequently entered service or took up apprenticeships which involved living away from home some time prior to reaching puberty. At the same time, males often delayed marriage and the establishment of an independent household until their mid- to late twenties. These practices, at a time when the average life span was somewhat shorter, meant that the semi-dependence of youth often covered a substantial proportion of the life cycle. In contrast, in Britain in the 1950s and 1960s, youth was often seen as synonymous with the teenage years: beginning at puberty and, for many, ending soon after they secured their first full-time jobs in their late teens.

During the 1960s and 1970s, young people's ability to make fairly direct school to work transitions made it possible to gain a degree of economic independence from the age of 15 or 16. Parents tended to expect young people to assume a degree of self-responsibility and economic independence on leaving full-time education (Chisholm 1990). Indeed, leaving education and collecting the first wage packet was symbolic for both young people and their parents and tended to be accompanied by the granting of greater freedoms and responsibilities (Kiernan 1992; Coles 1995). However, in late modernity, the sequencing of transitions and of key events in the life cycle of young people has changed (Krüger 1990). Whereas transitions in the 1950s and 1960s involved a sequence of events in which young people typically first left school, then had their first sexual encounter, left home and married sometime later, in modern Britain, young people tend to become sexually active prior to leaving school, they leave home earlier, yet marry and have children later.

Due to different patterns of educational participation in the 1960s and 1970s, working-class youth tended to become economically independent much earlier than those from the middle classes who often remained dependent on their parents until their early twenties (Roberts 1985). Although most teenagers continued to live in the family home, school-leavers were expected to make a contribution towards household expenses. At this time, even those who failed to find jobs were able to assume some financial independence through the ability to claim state benefits within a few weeks of leaving school. Although the level of financial aid was based on the assumption of some continued parental support, there was a recognition on the part of the state that school-leavers, as young adults, had a right to some economic autonomy at this stage in their lives. This principle was abandoned during the 1980s as the state increasingly relinquished economic responsibility for young people and forced parents to underwrite their offspring financially until their mid-twenties. Although strong class and gender-based differentials continue to exist in respect of routes followed from the age of 16, there are now few opportunities for young people to establish a relatively autonomous adult existence in their teenage years.

On a social policy level, a number of pieces of legislation were introduced during the 1980s which formalized this lengthening period of semi-dependency and, according to Jones (1995), effectively extended dependency to the age of 18 and semi-dependency to the age of 25. During this period, young people's relationship with the state is mediated by their parents and full citizenship is not conferred until they are able to assume a direct relationship to the state as independent adults (Jones and Wallace 1992). Prior to the 1986 Social Security Act, young people were able to claim supplementary benefit shortly after leaving full-time education.[1] Although 16- and 17-year-olds previously received reduced rate benefits, at 18 they qualified for the full adult rate, while those who left home before the age of 18 qualified for the full rate of housing and supplementary benefits. With the introduction of Income Support in 1988 and with subsequent amendments relating to 16- and 17-year-olds later in the same year, most young people under the age of 18 are disqualified from claiming income support even if they live away from home.[2] As a result of these changes, it has been estimated that 80,000 16- and 17-year-olds who have left full-time education had no source of income (Donoghue 1992). These changes not only affect 16- and 17-year-olds, under the new regulations young people do not receive the full benefit rate until the age of 25. With the replacement of unemployment benefit with the jobseekers allowance in 1996, 18–25-year-olds will be faced with a further £10 per week reduction in benefit which the government justifies through the claim that young people in this age group often live with their parents and have low wage expectations (Glennerster 1995; Murray 1996). While lone parents may be entitled to the full rate of income support at age 18, 16- and 17-year-olds only receive the standard rate for their age group rather than full 'adult' entitlements (Harris 1990). These legislative changes reflect the government's view that young people should be in full-time education or training and should not have the option of living off state benefits. It has also been argued that the changes were based on the view that families ought to assume financial responsibility for their offspring until they are able to stand on their own feet (Finch 1989).

This enforced lengthening of dependence in youth through the introduction of new legislation is not something which is peculiar to Britain, nor is it restricted to changes in the provision of state benefit. The Criminal Justice Act (1991) and the Criminal Justice and Public Order Act (1994), for example, require magistrates to bind over the parents or guardians of a child convicted of a criminal offence to 'exercise proper control' and ensure that they comply with any requirements of the court. Following legislative trends in the USA, the Labour party has stated an intention to consider the introduction of legally enforceable curfews for all young people. While full details of a British curfew have yet to be made available, in America curfews exist in 145 of the largest 200 cities (Allen-Mills 1996). In New Orleans, for example, young people under the age of 17 have to be off the streets by 8 p.m. in winter and 9 p.m. in summer. These changes highlight the extent to which structural changes have been reinforced by social policies so as to formalize the extension in the period of youth dependence in late modernity.

Identity

The extension in dependency that we have described has important implications for the establishment of identity. The social construction of youth in the modern period and the extension of dependency which has occurred over the last two decades is seen by some as providing a space in which young people can develop as individuals and experiment with different lifestyles in a context where the influence of the family is less prominent (Young 1987; Ainley 1991). However, others argue that these changes have had a negative impact on identity formation. For young people, the lengthening of the period between physical maturity and the attainment of adult status can be seen as problematic due to difficulties involved in constructing a stable identity in a period characterized by economic and social marginality. Youth is a period of uncertainty and where young people have no clear picture of what the future holds, this confusion can play a central role in the construction of identity. In this context, Côté and Allahar see adolescence in late modernity as characterized by an 'identity moratorium' which can have negative psychological consequences. Adolescence is a time of confusion in which some young people get lost or become sidetracked, as such youth can be the 'most destructive or wasted period of their lives' (1996: 74).

For much of this century, the establishment of adult identities was much more straightforward because of the speed with which transitions were completed, their relative simplicity, and because of the fairly stable nature of the occupational world. As we noted in the previous chapter, young people tended to follow clearly defined routes through the school and into the labour market, frequently following in the footsteps of their parents and older siblings. In these circumstances, identities tended to be developed in socially restricted networks and young people developed assumptive worlds which reflected established class and gender-based relationships. In late modernity, young people frequently lack these clear frames of reference and attempt to establish adult identities in a world which they perceive as filled with risk and uncertainty.

In an uncertain and rapidly changing social world, young people can find it difficult to construct stable social identities and are subject to an increasing range of social and cultural influences (Melucci 1992). In this respect, Côté and Allahar (1996) suggest that the identity crisis of youth in late modernity is socially produced with young people being particularly vulnerable to manipulation by adult profiteers. The mass media, for example, attempt to sell identity scripts which frequently involve stereotyped gender images. Leisure and youth cultures are also seen as having become much more central to an understanding of changing social identities among young people (see Chapter 5) and have implications for processes of individualization and risk.

Housing and domestic transitions

The protraction of the school to work transition, together with the legislative changes which we have described, have had an impact on young people's ability to make the housing and domestic transitions which are central to the attainment of adult status. As Coles (1995) notes, the three main transitions made by young people are closely interrelated and delays in the completion of one transition can have knock-on effects on other transitions. Over the last two decades, along with changes in school to work transitions, there have been important changes in the ways in which young people make their transitions from the parental home to independent living and the stage at which they establish their own families. Jones (1995) has argued that during the 1950s and 1960s domestic and housing transitions tended to occur very soon after completion of the school to work transition. This was particularly true for young people from working-class families who tended to leave the parental home, marry and have children relatively soon after entering the full-time labour market. From the 1970s, the spacing of the three transitions tended to widen, returning to a form which was common during the eighteenth and nineteenth centuries (Springhall 1986; Jones 1995).

Leaving home

Although young people today remain dependent on their families for longer than was the case two decades ago, the average age at which they first move away from the family home has declined (Kiernan 1986; Jones 1995). One of the reasons for this change is the increase in the number of young people who experience higher education (Kiernan 1986). For this reason, young people from middle-class families and those with strong academic credentials tend to move away from the parental home at a younger age than those from working-class families and those with poor academic qualifications (Young 1984; Jones 1987; Furlong and Cooney 1990). The age at which young people first move away from home is also affected by gender; females tend to leave sooner than males (Young 1984; Furlong and Cooney 1990; Jones 1995). This is partly because females are more likely to move away to study, but is also affected by their younger average age of marriage (Dunnell 1976; Young 1984; Jones 1987; Furlong and Cooney 1990). The younger age at which females tend to leave home has also been linked to the different ways in which parents treat daughters and sons; the behaviour of young women may be subject to closer scrutiny (Ward and Spitze 1992; White 1994) and they may be expected to provide a greater contribution to the household labour (White 1994). Although there has been little work on the domestic and housing transitions of members of ethnic minorities living in Britain, evidence from the USA suggests that due to the significance of extended families, irrespective of marital status, black youths are more likely to live with their parents (Hogan *et al.* 1990; White 1994).

According to White (1994), changes in patterns of residence among young people can be explained by economic, political and demographic factors. On an economic level, the availability of jobs and relative wages of young people are of crucial importance. In terms of recent trends, it can be argued that the shift from an industrial economy to one increasingly dominated by service industries (with a corresponding rise in the demand for educated workers) reduces young people's chances of establishing their independence at an early age. On a political level, the removal of entitlements to income support and housing benefit can also be seen as having an impact on housing and domestic transitions. Demographic factors, such as patterns of fertility, marriage and divorce also affect patterns of residence. An increase in the average age of marriage and childbearing may lead to delayed housing and family transitions, while the increased tendency for young people to experience the divorce of their parents may provide greater incentives to establish independent forms of residence.

In any discussion about young people's housing transitions, it is important to make the distinction between 'living away' and 'leaving home' (Jones 1987; Young 1987) as in Britain around a third of those who move away from home subsequently return (Kerckhoff and McRae 1992). Many students, for example, return to the family home after their college courses, and it is common for them to spend the long vacation in the family home. On the other hand, while young people from working-class families tend to leave home at an older age, their departure is more likely to be permanent (Young 1984; Jones 1987). In this context it is important to stress that although young people are tending to live away at a younger age than previously, it has become more common for them to return to the family home (Furlong and Cooney 1990), especially within a year or two of first leaving (Young 1989; White 1994). Females are less likely than males to return home; one of the reasons for this is that young women are more likely to leave home to marry (Goldscheider and DaVanzo 1986; Young 1989). For some commentators, housing transitions which include periods in which young people return to the family home have been interpreted as reflecting a disordered transition (Rindfuss *et al.* 1987), although others regard changes in residence as indicative of role transformations (such as that involved in completing a course of education) rather than of a failed transition (DaVanzo and Goldscheider 1990).

One of the reasons why young people are spending less time living with their parents or in independent households relates to the increased importance of 'intermediary households' (Penhale 1990; Irwin 1995; Jones 1995). Since the 1970s it has become increasingly common for young people to spend time living alone or with peers prior to making a domestic transition to marriage or cohabitation (Harris 1983; Young 1984; Jones 1995).

Experience of living in intermediary households has affected young people from both middle-class and working-class families, although there are important differences; among the middle classes, the transition to intermediary households tends to coincide with entry into higher education and involves living in student accommodation or sharing flats with peers. On the other hand, young people from working-class families are more likely to move into hostels, board with relatives or live in accommodation supplied by an employer (those joining the forces, for example, will live in military quarters, while those going into nursing may live in hospital accommodation) (Jones and Wallace 1992).

Young people move away from the family home for a variety of reasons; some leave to study or take up the offer of a job away from home, others leave to marry or to set up home with a partner. Others leave because of an uneasy coexistence with their parents, perhaps as a result of difficult relationships with parents or step-parents or due to domestic violence or abuse. Some are asked to leave or kicked out, and those leaving local authority care are required to set up independent households at a relatively young age (Coles 1995). As post-compulsory educational participation has increased, leaving home to attend college has become much more common (although there is evidence that an increasing proportion of students are applying to local colleges and universities in the face of the greater financial pressures on students). With employment prospects being greater in some parts of Britain, young people may also leave home for work-related reasons. Among young Scots who left home by the age of 19, Furlong and Cooney (1990) showed that nearly three in ten left in order to accept the offer of a job or to search for work in another area.

Although the data from the Scottish Young People's Survey shows that the proportion of young people leaving home due to various problems is small (16 per cent), Jones (1995) has argued that the numbers leaving home due to family problems has increased in recent years. In particular, the increase in divorce (since the 1960s there has been a four-fold increase in divorce; Burghes 1994), 'reconstituted families' and single parent families affects the stage at which young people make housing transitions and the level of support that they can expect. However, the association between reconstituted families (which are often regarded as less cohesive than natural families) and an early departure of young people from the family home tends to be stronger for females than males and more significant among whites and Asians than among Afro-Carribeans (Goldscheider and Goldscheider 1993). It has become more common for children to experience changes in family circumstances, spending time living as part of a single parent family or with step-parents (Haskey 1994), and Woodroffe and colleagues (1993) have shown that the number of children in lone parent families increased by 300 per cent between 1971 and 1989. Those growing up in reconstituted and single parent families tend to leave home at an earlier stage than those living with their natural parents (Ainley 1991; Kiernan 1992; Jones 1995).

Haskey (1994) argues that by the age of 16, around one in four young people will have experienced the divorce of their parents and many of these will spend time living in a reconstituted family. In a 1993 survey of 10,000 young Scots (SCEC 1994), 14 per cent of young people were found to be living with a single parent, 6 per cent were living with a step-parent and 2 per cent were living with grandparents or foster parents. Comparing data from the last two censuses, Ryan (1996) shows that between 1981 and 1991 the proportion of single parent families increased from 6.3 per cent to 13.9 per cent. Within deprived areas the rise has been more dramatic: from 9 per cent in 1981 to 22.5 per cent in 1991 with the proportion of single parent families in some areas being much higher (33.6 per cent in the London Borough of Lambeth, for example).

Although many children spend their entire childhoods in stable single parent families, Kiernan (1992) has argued that young people who have experienced the breakdown of their parents' marriages tend to make school to work transitions at an earlier stage. They also tend to have lower academic qualifications and an increased risk of unemployment (Wadsworth and Maclean 1986); this has implications for domestic and housing transitions. Jones (1995) reports that 40 per cent of males and 23 per cent of females who had previously lived with a step-parent gave 'family problems' as their main reason for leaving home. While new legislation requires families to assume greater financial support for those under the age of 25, increasingly young people come from family situations where such support is unlikely to be forthcoming. While these young people are under pressure to make rapid housing transitions, they do so under increasingly risky circumstances. Indeed, young people who leave home for work related reasons, to make domestic transitions or because of difficulties at home have tended to report economic problems such as difficulties managing money or finding accommodation (Furlong and Cooney 1990). Ainley suggests that moving away from home 'put virtually all young movers at an immediate material disadvantage' (1991: 108). Recent legislative changes which we have highlighted are likely to have exacerbated these problems.

Coles (1995) has also drawn attention to the relationship between accelerated housing careers and homelessness. In particular, he argues that those who spend time in care often find it difficult to successfully accomplish a housing transition and as a consequence they frequently become homeless and are overrepresented among the prison population. Although relatively few young people spend time in care, around one in four of the homeless population and nearly four out of ten prisoners have spent time in local authority care (Anderson *et al.* 1993; Coles 1995). There are few reliable statistics on changing patterns of homelessness among young people because those who are single tend not to register with local authorities for rehousing. The official trend in homelessness certainly underestimates the proportion of young people without a home, yet this figure increased from 53,000 in 1978 to 146,000 in 1990 (Woodroffe *et al.* 1993).[3] Recent estimates suggest that 156,000 young people under the age of 26 are homeless (Hill 1995).

Marriage and parenthood

Over the last two decades there has also been a greater separation of housing and domestic transitions with marriage and parenthood often being regarded as the 'definitive step to adulthood' (Kiernan 1986: 11). Ainley (1991) argues that domestic transitions are a particularly significant step in the attainment of full adult status due to an underlying shift in responsibilities: the young adult is no longer the responsibility of their parents and comes to assume responsibility for others. During the 1960s, marriage was often the principal reason for leaving home and in many working-class communities it was 'almost unheard of for young people to leave home prior to marriage' (Leonard 1980: 61). However, while the age at which young people first move away from home has declined, the age of marriage has increased and the link between leaving the parental home and marriage has weakened (Jones 1995).

Between 1970 and 1993, the average age at first marriage increased by four years for both males and females (from 24 to 28 years for males and from 22 to 26 years for females) (CSO 1972, 1996). Moreover, while in 1971 9 per cent of young women married while they were in their teens, by 1992 less than 1 per cent of females married within their teenage years (CSO 1995a). Females have tended to marry at an earlier age than males, those whose parents have divorced and those who live with step-parents tend to marry early (Kiernan 1992); and class-based differences in the average age of marriage and childbearing have been observed throughout the century. The mean age of marriage among young women from unskilled manual backgrounds, for example, is 22, compared to 26 among those from professional and managerial families. Across all social classes, the average period of time between marriage and birth of the first child has increased over the last two decades, while the fertility rates of young women under the age of 25 have fallen (CSO 1996) (Figure 4.1), the average age at which women have their

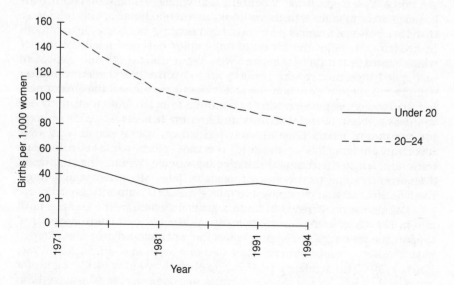

Figure 4.1   Fertility rates, by age: 1971–94
Source: CSO 1996

first child being 23.7 among those from semi- and unskilled backgrounds, compared to 27.9 among those from professional and managerial families.

Single parenthood and welfare dependency

Although the evidence seems to suggest that domestic transitions now tend to occur at a much later stage, one of the key changes over the last two decades has been the increase in cohabitation. Haskey and Kiernan (1989) show that among women who married in 1987, more than half had cohabited with their partners prior to marriage. This compares to just over a third of those who married in 1980 and just 8 per cent of those marrying in 1970. In 1989, more than six in ten (62 per cent) 16- to 19-year-olds who were living with a partner were not married, the corresponding figure for 1980 was just 13 per cent. Similarly, for 20- to 24-year-olds, the rate of cohabitation among couples increased from 11 per cent to 32 per cent (Kiernan and Estaugh 1993). Births outside marriage more than doubled between 1977 and 1993, with young women from working-class families being twice as likely to have a child outside marriage than those from the middle classes (Babb and Bethare 1995). However, many 'illegitimate' children are born to parents in stable relationships and the birth is jointly registered by two parents living at the one address (Hess 1995). Furthermore, young mothers frequently marry soon after the birth of their babies (Hess 1995).

The increase in the numbers of young women having children outside of marriage has recently been the focus of media attention and political debate. Indeed, one of the reasons for the removal of housing benefit from the under 25 age group was a concern that young people were abusing the benefit system to make transitions from the parental home at an earlier stage than their personal finances permitted: rapid housing and domestic transitions being characteristic of the period of full employment and relative affluence which existed in the 1960s (Kiernan 1985). While rising youth unemployment in the 1970s reduced young people's access to the independent resources which would permit early housing and domestic transitions, the government felt that young people were able to continue to make these transitions due to the availability of social security and housing benefits. In terms of housing transitions, media attention was focused on young people who were reportedly enjoying 'life on the dole' in seaside resorts, while early domestic transitions led to the accusation that young women were having children at a younger age due to the lack of available jobs. Moreover, young single mothers were seen as 'jumping the queue' for local authority housing.

While national trends indicate a general decline in the teenage birth rate in periods of rising unemployment (Ainley 1991), there is evidence to support the view that young people who are unemployed are more likely to have children than those in full-time jobs or education (Coffield *et al.* 1986; Harris 1990). This tendency has been explained in terms of the desire for status and independence among a group of young people who have been denied access to other sources of fulfilment in the form of opportunities for jobs or education (Coffield *et al.* 1986; Wallace 1987; Banks and Ullah 1988).

In other words, parenthood can provide a source of identity for young people who are marginalized in other life contexts.

Rather than being seen as a consequence of rapid labour market change and of a decline in demand for unskilled young workers (Gallie 1994), an increase in births outside of marriage and subsequent labour market withdrawal has often been presented as indicative of a culture of welfare dependency and weak labour market commitment (Murray 1990). In this context, the increase in the numbers of single mothers existing on welfare benefits has also been linked to concerns that children are being socialized into a dependency culture. As Bagguley and Mann argue,

> the focus on single mothers emphasizes their marital status and long-term dependence on public welfare. It is then assumed that they inculcate their offspring with the idea that welfare dependency carries no stigma or material disadvantage. From this it is claimed that the next generation are less willing or able to escape.
>
> (1992: 122)

Bagguley and Mann argue that with many children from welfare dependent homes managing to make successful labour market transitions, the empirical evidence does not lend support to the idea that there is a self-perpetuating underclass characterized by a cultural commitment to continued welfare dependency. Indeed, the increase in young single parents who are dependent on welfare benefits is more likely to reflect the economic difficulties faced by young mothers in a period characterized by low youth wages and a declining demand for unskilled youth labour.

Conclusion

In some respects, it can be argued that recent changes in domestic and housing transitions reflect an increase in the range of possibilities open to young people. The extension and desequencing of transitions has been seen by some as helping to create the space in which young people can experiment with different forms of living and establish a self-identity in a context where they are free from some of the constraints which shaped the experiences of the previous generation. However, we have suggested that in late modernity young people face difficulties in constructing stable social identities and that these problems will be reflected in different dimensions of their lives. These differences will be explored in subsequent chapters.

Two decades ago, young people from working-class families tended to leave home in order to establish a marital household and parental responsibilities were assumed at a relatively early age. Housing and domestic transitions were frequently made simultaneously and residence with peers, cohabitation and independent living were patterns largely reserved for middle-class youth. With the protraction of domestic and housing transitions and with increasing levels of post-compulsory educational participation, today there are more similarities between the experiences of working-class and middle-class youths and between young men and women. By the 1990s, most young people first left home for reasons other than marriage and the desire to establish the basis for independent lifestyles had become particularly significant (Poole 1989).

Yet while these changes can be seen as reflecting a process of individualization through which young people are presented with a greater range of choices, domestic and housing transitions remain highly structured. The timing of transitions and the ease with which they are made are largely determined by the individual's social location and the risks associated with unsuccessful transitions are not distributed in an equal fashion. Indeed, we suggest that many recent social policies have resulted in an increased dependence of youths on their families in a period when the family as an institution is undergoing some fundamental changes. The extension of dependency, which has been enforced by legislation, runs counter to the demands for greater autonomy that come from both young people and their parents (Harris 1990). The legislation rests on the dubious assumption that families are able and willing to support their offspring until the age of 25 and that young people are willing to submit to the authority of their parents during this period. As a consequence of these changes, we suggest that many of the most vulnerable young people are subject to new risks and uncertainties.

Notes

1 The 1986 Social Security Act was implemented in 1988.
2 Young people remain eligible for severe hardship payments and bridging allowances.
3 There are various definitions of homelessness which range from sleeping rough to living in temporary accommodation.

5 Leisure *and* lifestyles

> We are uncertain whether to dispute earlier theories of youth culture
> or to announce a major historical change. Whatever the earlier
> situation, our evidence shows that by the end of the 1980s in Britain
> young people's levels and types of leisure activity and sociability were
> not reflecting class divisions in the ways that formally applied, or were
> alleged to apply in certain frequently cited texts.
>
> (Roberts and Parsell 1994: 33)

Introduction

During the last two decades, changes in patterns of educational participation, delayed labour market transitions and an extension in the period of dependency have all had implications for the lifestyles which young people adopt and for the ways in which they spend their free time. Although leisure and lifestyles continue to reflect gender and, to a lesser extent, class locations, there is evidence that these divisions have blurred as a consequence of the influence of leisure industries and the common experience of delayed transitions (Roberts and Parsell 1994).[1] Males and females from all social classes tend to have more free time than previously and engage in a greater range of leisure pursuits. Young people tend to marry and have children at a later age, and this again increases the period of their lives in which they have a relatively high discretionary element to their spending (Stewart 1992). Moreover, changing transitional patterns have led to a greater equalization in levels of disposable income among young people under the age of 20 from different social classes (Stewart 1992).

These changes have resulted in new freedoms as well as constraints. In late modernity, people are faced with a greater range of choices in many different aspects of their lives, yet at the same time they remain subject to a powerful set of constraints and influences (Clarke and Critcher 1985). This contradiction is particularly evident in the closely linked spheres of leisure and consumption.[2] In the 1990s, young people are able to select from a wide range of leisure pursuits and through the development of specific modes of consumption are encouraged to adopt styles which highlight their individuality. At the same time, the media and leisure and consumption industries play a central role in the post-industrial economy and, through the use of advanced marketing strategies, large corporations are able to shape the preferences of consumers (Clarke and Critcher 1985; Langman 1992). Indeed, Clarke and Critcher (1985) argue that rather than being shaped through individual choice or fashion, leisure is a product of the class struggle and tends to be shaped by the dominant class. Similarly, Bourdieu (1986) recognizes that there are ongoing struggles over leisure and lifestyles and that dominant definitions are frequently resisted.

The greater diversification and individualization of style, leisure and consumption which are evident in late modernity can be seen as indicative of a new set of constraints which stem from advanced marketing techniques. Rojek (1985) has argued that within modern capitalism four trends can be identified; privatization, individuation, commercialization and pacification. Leisure has become increasingly privatized in so far as the widespread ownership of home-based entertainment systems such as television and video have helped transform leisure from a public to a private form of activity. The individuation of leisure is linked to the commercial development of leisure as a commodity which helps to define individual lifestyles. The commercialization of leisure is reflected in the dominance of large corporations who organize their highly profitable businesses in ways which shape demand and manipulate patterns of use. The process of pacification highlights the ways in which leisure can be portrayed as a process of social control, providing a mechanism through which social integration can be maintained in a society characterized by an increasing division of labour and diverse life experiences.

It is in the context of these debates about leisure and lifestyles in the age of late modernity that we will assess Beck's claim that people are now constrained to assert their individuality and creativity through modes of consumption and associated lifestyles. In our view, trends in leisure highlight the ways in which the epistemological fallacy of high modernity is sustained. The blurring of class and gender divisions in leisure, which arise in part from processes of commercialization, help create an illusion of individuality and classlessness. Social identities are partly shaped through lived experiences in the related spheres of leisure and consumption and any weakening of class divisions in these fields will therefore be manifest in the ways in which people subjectively locate themselves in the social world. In this respect our views come close to those members of the Frankfurt school (Horkheimer and Adorno 1972), who suggested that the culture industry can be regarded as a source of ideological manipulation.

We begin this chapter by describing some of the ways in which young people's leisure and lifestyles have changed and later return to examine the extent to which we can regard these changes as representing an individualization of leisure and lifestyle. Through an analysis of changing youth cultures we also look at the influence of peer groups and at the way in which fashions are subject to constraints of the market. We suggest that despite an outward appearance of diversity and choice young people can increasingly be seen as constrained within a 'neon cage' (Langman 1992) of consumerism which blinds them to the underlying realities which condition their social existence.

Leisure

Young people spend their free time in many different ways; while some spend much of their leisure time in informal pursuits or solitary activities, others participate in a range of organized and group activities. Despite the variety of activities, there are distinct patterns in the range and types of activities in which young people engage. Many studies of young people's leisure activities have highlighted the maintenance of strong gender divisions which are often seen as more significant than class or differences associated with 'race' (Gratton and Taylor 1985; Roberts *et al.* 1989; Furlong *et al.* 1990). It has been noted that girls are less leisure-active than boys; they are expected to spend more of their free time helping out in the home and are often required to return home earlier in the evening. Moreover, they tend to have fewer resources to help enrich their leisure time; they receive lower wages and less pocket money and have higher 'self-maintenance costs' (Roberts 1983).

In an analysis of the relationship between post-16 experiences and the leisure patterns of 19-year-olds, Furlong and colleagues (1990) argued that transitional patterns had important implications for young people's leisure experiences. In particular, they suggested that extended education and delays in entering full-time employment provided young people with different leisure opportunities, as well as new restrictions. Young people who remained in full-time education tended to report the highest overall level of leisure activity, while those who were unemployed participated in fewest activities. Yet irrespective of the transitional routes followed by young people, strong differences were evident between males and females.

Over the last two decades there have been changes in the leisure patterns of young women, yet gender has remained a strong predictor of participation in 'active' pursuits (Glyptis 1989); in particular, boys tend to go out more often, are more likely to engage in vigorous exercise and participate in sports (Furlong *et al.* 1990; Woodroffe *et al.* 1993). Hendry and colleagues (1993) argue that many leisure settings are male preserves and that this lack of access to leisure space for girls means that they often retreat into home-based activities where they can spend time with a small group of close friends (McRobbie and Garber 1976) and develop what Frith (1978) refers to as a 'bedroom culture'. Focusing on sports participation, Hendry and colleagues (1993) found that among 13- to 20-year-olds, around three-quarters of boys but less than half of the girls participated in sports on a weekly basis. However, since the late 1970s the gap between men's and women's sports participation has narrowed slightly (Glyptis 1989; Roberts *et al.* 1990).

The lower levels of sports participation among young women partly reflects a tendency to dislike collective team activities as well as concerns relating to the compatibility of sports with their perceptions of womanhood. Hendry and colleagues (1993) suggest that female cultures tend to emphasize 'best friends' and close relationships with small groupings and that this results in a general discomfort with collective team situations. Coakley and White (1992) argue that boys regard sporting activity as congruent with the masculine role and gain kudos from engaging in competitive and aggressive leisure activities. On the other hand, girls tend not to connect sports activity with the process of becoming a woman and may avoid participating in leisure activities which may be perceived as threatening to their femininity. These differences have important implications. Women are often prevented from competing with men, and through this process of segregation sports can

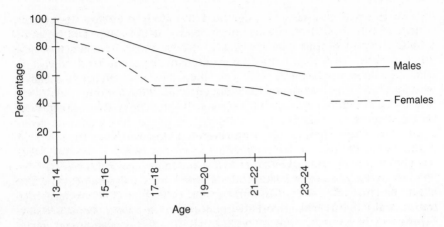

Figure 5.1 Weekly involvement in sport
Source: Hendry *et al*. 1993

be seen as converting 'physical differences into cultural definitions of super-
iority and inferiority, ensuring that women come off second best' (Clarke and
Critcher 1985: 162).

Throughout adolescence, young people's involvement in sporting activities decline and girls tend to turn their backs on sports at an earlier stage
than males (Figure 5.1) (Hendry *et al*. 1993). Smith (1987) found that at the
age of 11–12 both boys and girls tended to prefer sports to other activities,
but while boys tended to chose a team game, girls often selected more individualized activities such as swimming. Indeed, the favoured leisure activities
of males in this age group were social, while girls tended to choose individualistic pursuits. At age 13–14, boys still emphasized team games while girls
started to place less emphasis on individual activities and tended to develop
a stronger interest in social activities, dancing and music. By the age of 15–
16, both males and females started to place a greater emphasis on social
activities, although boys retained their interest in team games.

In this context, Rapoport and Rapoport (1975) argued that for young
people, the life cycle was marked by two phases in leisure activity: the first
(between the ages of 15 and 19) involving exploration and a quest for
personal identity, the second (from about 16 to 26) involving the establishment of a social identity and the formation of relationships. In a later and
more detailed analysis of young people and leisure, Hendry and colleagues
(1993) argued that the leisure patterns of both boys and girls move through
three age-related stages: 'organized leisure', 'casual leisure' and 'commercial
leisure' with boys making transitions from one phase to the next at a later
age than girls. Organized leisure includes sports participation which tends to
decline from the ages of 13 to 14. Casual leisure includes hanging around
with friends, and this tends to be less common after the age of 16. Commercial leisure becomes the predominant form after the age of 16 and includes
cinema attendance as well as visiting discos and pubs: on average, 75 per

cent of 16- to 24-year-olds, for example, visit pubs four times a week (Willis 1990). Within the commercial leisure stage, young people start to spend greater amounts of time in mixed gender environments, time which accord-ing to Clarke and Critcher is 'charged with sexual promise' (1985: 162). In this sense, the word commercial takes on a double meaning with young people acting as consumers in a sexual market place in which 'wares are displayed, consumer choices made, sexuality bartered' (Clarke and Critcher 1985: 163).

At all stages, women's leisure participation is constrained by gender rela-tions (Talbot 1979; Deem 1986; Wearing and Wearing 1988; Green *et al.* 1990; Henderson 1991). In particular, leisure opportunities are restricted through conventions governing the use of space. There are a number of restrictions regarding the use of space which inhibit women's freedom of access (Townsend 1991), restrictions which also apply to members of ethnic minorities and which may be enforced more strongly in Muslim and Hindu cultures. It has been argued, for example, that when girls want to participate in a sport, they often need to involve a friend or relative before it is considered safe or appropriate. Coakley and White (1992) cite conventions which tend to pre-vent young women entering snooker halls alone, while accepting women who accompany a boyfriend or brother as spectators. In contrast, there are fewer conventions which restrict the activities of young males.

In a study of women's leisure participation in two contrasting areas of Tyneside, Mowl and Towner (1994) found that despite strong differ-ences between the areas, women's fear of violence represented a common constraint.

> No matter where women live on Tyneside, whether 'local' or 'non-local', middle class or working class, young or old, employed or not, all women have their leisure behaviour constrained by a common factor: the fear of male violence in public space.
>
> (1994: 120)

They argued that 'women's leisure opportunities whether real or perceived are conditioned by local patriarchal relations which are reproduced in the home, workplace and community' (1994: 105). A number of other writers have also highlighted the ways in which women's fear of public spaces, especially after dark, represent an important constraint on their leisure activities outside the home (Deem 1986; Green *et al.* 1990).

Although the gendering of social space has an impact on the range of activities in which young women become engaged, participation in many home-based leisure pursuits also varies by gender (with the exception of watching television and videos and listening to the radio and popular music). Males are more likely to report spending time using a home computer, while females are more likely to read literature and poetry and listen to classical music (Furnham and Gunter 1989). Figures from the General Household Survey (OPCS 1995) support these findings and also show that young males are more likely to spend time on DIY projects and gardening, while females spend time dressmaking and knitting. In terms of gender differences in leisure activities, little change in patterns of participation over the last decade could be detected from figures reported in the General Household Survey. However, Roberts and colleagues (1990) have argued that gender-based differences in leisure pursuits have become narrower. For example, differences in levels of sports participation have narrowed in recent years, and males and females are equally likely to spend time in pubs.

Using data from a survey of 19-year-old Scots, Roberts and colleagues argued that by the late 1980s there was little evidence to suggest that young women were leading narrower leisure lives than males. After calculating range and frequency of participation in a variety of activities, they argued that young women had slightly higher overall activity rates. Male leisure, they suggested, tended to be 'more locked within a narrow masculine track dominated by sport and drink' (1990: 131). Yet males and females engaged in a highly gendered set of activities. Males tended to be more likely to play or watch sport, while females were more likely to go out for meals, read books and magazines, go to cinemas, theatres, concerts and churches and visit friends and relations. Importantly, gender differences in leisure behaviour are lowest among those who remain in full-time education the longest, perhaps reflecting access to institutional facilities which may be perceived by females as safe (Roberts *et al.* 1990).

The leisure lifestyles of young people also continue to be affected by social class with middle-class youths being more culturally active than those from working-class families. In a recent Australian study, Garton and Pratt (1991) tried to ascertain the extent to which the leisure interests expressed by young people were related to external constraints and processes. They concluded that while the major predictor of the recreational leisure activities of school students was gender, interests were also determined by the availability of resources. Middle-class youths are more likely to attend the theatre and cinema, with over half seeing a film every month compared to around a third of working-class youth (Reimer 1995). Data from the General Household Survey (OPCS 1995) also shows the extent to which sports participation varies by social class. In 1993, 64 per cent of those from the professional classes had participated in sports or games in the previous four weeks, compared to 31 per cent of the unskilled manual class. Since the late 1980s, levels of sports participation had increased generally, but this had no effect on class differentials (OPCS 1995).

Despite suggestions that the relationship between class and leisure activities has weakened, the range of choices and decisions about leisure participation continues to be influenced both by class cultures and young people's access to material resources (Coakley and White 1992). Those from working-class families tend to lack resources to participate in certain activities, but they can also be reluctant to participate in activities they associate with the middle classes due to a fear of ridicule. Indeed, Coakley and White suggest that 'the decision to participate in sport was integrally tied to the way young people viewed themselves and their connection in the social world' (1992: 32).

Although there is still an association between social class and young people's leisure lifestyles, it is possible that ongoing changes in young people's experiences will lead to a process of homogenization. Roberts and Parsell, for example, have argued that one of the consequences of extended transitions will be 'the blurring of class-related leisure patterns' as young people from across the social spectrum increasingly share leisure tastes and milieux (1992a: 747). However, while Furlong and colleagues (1990) also note that the trend towards longer participation in education may broaden the leisure horizons of working-class youth, they argue that other trends (such as the concentration of unemployment and scheme participation among the working classes) may counteract the impact of educational changes. Young people with low educational attainments (who are predominantly from working-class families), are particularly vulnerable to unemployment (Gray *et al.* 1983; Ashton 1986; White and McRae 1989) and those who spend time out of work tend to lead narrow and unfulfilling leisure lifestyles. Unemployed youths lack the resources to participate in commercial leisure activities (at a time when these are becoming much more central to the lives of their peers in employment and education) and tend to spend greater amounts of time hanging around (Hendry and Raymond 1983). Indeed, as Hendry and colleagues suggest, 'a major consequence of unemployment is to deny young people entry to the "package" of work and leisure which is integral to "adult" lifestyle' (1993: 54).

Youth cultures

As well as having an impact on the use of leisure time, changing transitional experiences, together with more aggressive and sophisticated marketing techniques, have also affected young people's lifestyles and the patterns of consumption which tend to symbolize cultural identification. Young people now spend a longer period of time in a state of semi-dependency and in the company of their peers and this has had an impact on the styles they adopt and the groups and products with which they identify. Yet while there was once a close correspondence between fashions and class membership, there is evidence that the relationship between youth cultures and class has weakened (McRobbie 1993; Roberts and Parsell 1994). In particular, in the fields of fashion and popular music, the once dominant influence of working-class youth has declined and the middle classes have become increasingly influential (Frith 1978; Roberts and Parsell 1994). These changes, which probably reflect changes in class-related income differentials stemming from the collapse of the youth labour market, are regarded as significant in so far as youth cultures have been regarded as a barometer of future social change (Widdicombe and Woffitt 1995).

The idea that the relationship between class and youth culture is now weak contrasts quite strongly with ideas being advanced by members of the Centre for Contemporary Cultural Studies in the 1970s (Cohen 1972; Hall and Jefferson 1976; Hebdige 1979). Hebdige (1979), for example, argued that through visual style, young people expressed their resistance to authority. In particular, youth cultures were seen as class-based and providing an arena in which young people sought generational solutions to political questions (Hollands 1990). During the 1950s and 1960s, youth cultures were seen as having their roots in the working class (Roberts 1983; Roberts and Parsell 1994). The predominant styles of the time, teddy boys, mods and rockers, were seen as adaptations of working-class cultures and middle-class youth were largely excluded. Working-class youth, for example, were responsible for the growing popularity of rock and roll in the 1950s. In this context, Murdock and McCron (1976) have argued that there was a strong connection between musical tastes and class.

During the 1960s the situation began to change; middle-class youths, who once had little involvement in youth cultures, started to develop their own styles revolving around 'progressive rock' music and radical politics. By the late 1960s, musical tastes and youth styles had begun to cross class boundaries. Douvan and Adelson (1966) argued that popular music had been responsible for a homogenization of youth cultures in the US, while in Britain the popularity of the Beatles and the 1960s British pop scene was also seen as helping to dilute the significance of class divisions among young people (Murdock and McCron 1976). From this stage onwards, the association between class and youth styles started to weaken, changes which were resented by skinheads who attempted to re-establish a traditional working-class youth culture in a period characterized by a decline in working-class communities and manual employment. Despite resistance by some groups, by the 1990s, Roberts and Parsell were arguing that 'virtually all leisure activities and types of sociability linked rather than separated young people in different class locations' (1994: 33).

Since the emergence of distinct youth cultures during the 1950s, young people's lifestyles have frequently been portrayed as threatening and as posing a 'challenge to the symbolic order which guarantees their subordination' (Hebdige 1988: 18). Groups as diverse as teddy boys, mods, rockers, hippies, Rastas, punks and skinheads have all been used by the press to generate moral panics over youth cultures and their threat to 'civilized' society. Widdicombe and Woffitt see teddy boys as particularly significant as reactions to them 'set the scene for public, media and academic concern with subsequent youth cultures' (1995: 8). In the 1960s, mods and rockers were portrayed as violent hooligans, while left wing and anarchist philosophies of hippies and student activists were seen as representing a more direct threat to the political order. The latest threat to symbolic order is the raver, with some writers interpreting acid house as an expression of dissatisfaction with Thatcherite philosophy (Russell 1993).

The emergence of youth cultures in the post-war period can be linked to economic changes. Their development is closely linked to the relative affluence of youth and the ways in which they have been targeted by the fashion and music industries. From the mid-1950s, in the affluent post-war years, teenagers started to be regarded as forming a specific market niche with distinctive purchasing styles and patterns of consumption (Abrams 1961; Davis 1990). Davis (1990) argued that by the late 1950s the average teenage earnings had increased by more than 50 per cent in real terms compared to the pre-war levels. The post-war boom meant that young workers had relatively high wages compared to their pre-war counterparts and in real terms their contribution to the household economy fell (Stewart 1992). Young people's spending tended to be concentrated in 'non-essential' sectors and this made them a target for the growing leisure industry (Abrams 1961) and led to the formation of a specialized youth market, supplying goods and services ranging from fashion and entertainment to food and drink.

Table 5.1 The spending priorities of 16–24-year-olds: 1990

Item	%
Clothes	68
Records/tapes/music	34
Going out/drinking	21
Save towards holiday/special purchase	20
Something for car/motorbike	13
Cosmetics/haircare products	8
Books	7
Sport	7
Hobbies	7

Source: Stewart 1992

Between the 1950s and 1990s, the spending habits of young people have been remarkably stable with the bulk of their expenditure being concentrated on clothes and music (Stewart 1992) (Table 5.1). In this context it is important to stress the ways in which changing styles have been manipulated by the marketing strategies of large firms. Indeed, Ferchoff (1990) has argued that in Germany youth cultures and styles are not so much related to specific class cultures, but should be regarded as commercialized and incorporated forms with cultural styles being packaged and marketed to a wider section of the young population. Acid house, for example, began as a small subculture but elements were rapidly absorbed by mainstream youth culture. Similarly, punk originated as the antithesis of commercial youth fashion, but the style was eventually marketed to a wider population. In this context, Willis (1990) describes how the leggings worn by punk girls were originally purchased as cream coloured items of thermal underwear and dyed black. By the mid-1980s, commercial manufacturers were producing coloured leggings for the mass market and they had become standard apparel for a broad age range of women.

In late modernity, the visual styles adopted by young people through the consumption of clothing are regarded as having become increasingly central to the establishment of identity and to peer relations (Miles 1996). While traditional sources of social differentiation based on social class and communities are thought to have weakened, young people are seen as attempting to find self-fulfilment and ways of identifying with other young people through their consumption of goods, especially fashion (Willis 1990; Miles 1995). In this context, Kellner argues that whereas identity was previously shaped in occupational settings, in late modernity 'identity revolves around leisure, centred on looks, images and consumption' (1992: 153). Indeed, for

Beck (1992) individual consumer choices and styles are something which have been created through marketing strategies and the media. In turn, 'consumer styles and artefacts come to be perceived as an integral part of [young people's] identity' (Jones and Wallace 1992: 119).

For commercial organizations, the value of youths as consumers should not be underestimated. As part of an attempt to remarket Levi 501 jeans following low sales in the 1970s and early 1980s, £10 million was dedicated to a television and cinema advertising campaign which helped increase sales from 80,000 in 1985 to 650,000 in 1986 (Tomlinson 1990). Football teams have also generated large incomes through the marketing of football shirts and through introducing new designs on a yearly basis. Newcastle United, for example, sold an estimated 400,000 shirts in one year (Guardian 1995). In this context, Miles (1996) argues that it is necessary to focus on the meanings young people attach to the goods that they purchase and the ways in which young people communicate and establish shared values through tastes in fashion.

For Miles (1995, 1996), patterns of youth consumption are seen as central to the social construction of identity. With the decline of the youth labour market, young people are increasingly turning to the market place to purchase props for their identity, which can make them more confident in their relationships with their peers. In late modernity, patterns of consumption and leisure lifestyles have also been regarded as central to the establishment of masculine and feminine identities (Hollands 1995). Yet youth styles can often be seen as highlighting similarity rather than difference; 'street cred' comes from conforming to dominant fashions rather than being an expression of individuality. The themes of confidence and conformity come across strongly in the work of Miles (1995), as expressed here by Darren and Tony:

> *Darren:* Name brands give you confidence and that. If you like what you're wearing, if you think you've spent a lot of money on it like, it gives you a lot of confidence.
>
> *Tony:* I'm forever buying stuff just because I've seen it on someone else. I try it on and see if it looks good on me. Then you buy it. It might look rubbish on you, but everyone's wearing it.

For young people growing up in the 1990s and increasingly excluded from paid employment, their relationship to the means of consumption is probably more significant than traditional class differences in explaining cultural identification. Those who have access to the necessary resources are able to participate in youth cultures which cross-cut class boundaries. At the same time, it is important to recognize that obscurity of class boundaries and the illusion of choice masks the powerful commercial interests which shape both lifestyles and identity. Indeed, Côté and Allahar argue that young people have been manipulated by commercial concerns and sold identities which are 'illusory and fleeting', processes which have led to 'an epidemic of socially produced identity crises in advanced industrial societies' (1996: xvii). The centrality of consumption in shaping the identities of young people has also been interpreted by Seabrook as 'a subtle and less readily discernible bondage' for the working classes. Young people are seen as 'trapped, function-less and without purpose', locked into an acquisitive culture of yearning for material possessions. The 'primary determinant' in their lives is 'a lopsided insistence on buying, getting, having', representing 'an even greater subjection than has been known before' (Seabrook 1983: 8–11).

Although there is evidence that class has weakened as a predictor of youth styles and social identities, there are still important differences in access to lifestyles which can be explained on a material level. While some young people have access to resources which will allow them to participate fully in the predominant patterns of youth consumption, others find them-selves marginalized and excluded. In addition to financial exclusion, the un-employed may become culturally excluded as they lack the means to sustain 'appropriate' cultural identities. Jones and Wallace (1992), for example, argue that even those on low incomes are under pressure to purchase clothes which emphasize a particular style, while those who are excluded from the process of consumption are portrayed as 'weak-willed and unable to exploit their freedom' (Tomlinson 1990: 13). Difficulties in securing legitimate access to culturally valued fashion accessories may lead young people to seek altern-ative (illegal) means of satisfying their desires (see Chapter 7).

Conclusion

With the extension of youth as a stage in the life cycle and with a growing range of possible activities in which young people can engage, the lives of the younger generation in Britain have changed significantly. Of the changes that have taken place, the one which perhaps casts most light on the charac-teristics of life in high modernity concerns the apparent weakening of social class as a predictor of leisure and lifestyles among young people. Many young people now spend their immediate post-school years on training schemes, and differences in the spending power of those following educational routes and those leaving school at an early stage to enter training have become narrower. Although gender differences remain powerful, there is evidence that they have weakened and, with the narrowest gender differences being observed in those following educational routes, we can perhaps expect this trend to continue.

While youth cultures now tend to cross-cut traditional class divisions and with patterns of leisure having become less differentiated, it is apparent that some young people have been marginalized. Indeed, the most signific-ant differences in leisure and lifestyles become apparent when we look at the situation faced by the unemployed. Those without jobs are denied access to the rich leisure lifestyles enjoyed by the majority of today's youth. Moreover, in settings which have become increasingly commercialized, the unemployed are excluded from the consumer culture which is central to the shaping of young people's identity in the modern world. Exclusion from consumer cultures can reduce young people's confidence and prevent their acceptance within a youth culture which cross-cuts class divisions.

These changes in young people's leisure and lifestyles highlight the implications of the process of individualization identified by Beck (1992). Young people are often able to choose between a wide range of activities and construct their identities in an arena where the impact of traditional social divisions appears weak. Yet the obscurity of class in these crucial life contexts has powerful implications for social life in general. Indeed, the lived and mediated experiences of young people in the fields of leisure and consumption is an important mechanism via which the epistemological fallacy of late modernity is maintained and reproduced.

Notes

1 Sociologists have defined leisure in a variety of ways. Here we adopt one of the most common definitions in which leisure is equated with time which is free from other obligations (Roberts 1983; Rojek 1985).
2 Given that most leisure activities are commercialized and involve monetary exchange, we regard leisure and consumption as being closely linked.

6 Health risks *in* late modernity

One of the human prices paid for the current economic condition is the widespread loss of confidence in the future felt by working class youth . . . drug dependency, mental illness, even suicide; these are all symptoms of the changes experienced by youth.

(Cashmore 1984: vii)

Introduction

The protraction of the school to work transition, changes in domestic and housing transitions, as well as the commercialization of leisure and lifestyles which have been described in previous chapters, have all led to new forms of risk and vulnerability. In this chapter we highlight some of the main health risks faced by young people growing up in modern Britain and examine the extent to which the distribution of these risks reflect what Beck would regard as 'traditional' inequalities. While many of the health risks encountered by young people are still differentially distributed along the lines of class and gender, we suggest that processes of individualization, coupled with the stress which develops out of uncertain transitional outcomes, have implications for the health of all young people. In particular, it is argued that the protraction and desequencing of youth transitions have had a negative impact on young people's mental health. In this respect, Beck and Giddens are correct to suggest that reflexive individualization, together with the need to establish adult identities and sustain coherent narratives in a rapidly changing social world, can lead to new risks.

Youth has traditionally been portrayed as a period of exploration and experimentation and youth styles sometimes involve risks which can adversely affect the health of young people and even lead to premature death. While some of the physical risks associated with youthful activities may not have changed much over the last twenty years, we suggest that the changing transitional experiences of young people have led to a generalized increase in stress which is reflected in a rise in suicide, attempted suicide (parasuicide), and eating disorders such as anorexia and bulimia. In addition, there are many health risks faced by young people which are related to their everyday experiences; smoking, social drinking and sexual discovery, for example, are central experiences in the lives of young people which can have harmful consequences. In this chapter we attempt to put some of these risks into perspective and show the ways in which the vulnerability of youth may have changed.

Health inequalities in youth

Youth and early adulthood are frequently portrayed as periods in which young people reach a peak in terms of general health and physical fitness. Compared to earlier and later stages in the life cycle, few young people suffer from acute or life threatening conditions. The risks posed by congenital and infectious diseases during childhood (such as respiratory and heart conditions) are reduced, while degenerative diseases (such as heart conditions and cancer) tend to pose minimal threats (Hurrelmann 1990; Kutcher 1994). In the late teenage years, injuries and poisoning are the main causes of death, while road accidents account for the largest proportion of deaths from injuries (Woodroffe *et al.* 1993). As Hurrelmann argues, it is misleading to portray adolescence as a period characterized by an absence of health risks; accidental death, suicide and violent crime are central to an understanding of health risks in adolescence, together with sexual disease, mental disorders, the consequences of early pregnancy, and drug abuse. Moreover, many aspects of young people's lifestyles and behaviours have longer term consequences for their health, such as smoking, alcohol abuse and the lack of exercise.

The myth of a healthy adolescence is reflected in the lack of research specifically addressing the epidemiology of youth. Indeed, some of the most comprehensive and influential studies of health, such as the Black Report (Townsend and Davidson 1982), have used such wide age bands that youth has been rendered invisible (West 1988, forthcoming). It is clear, however, that while in childhood girls are healthier than boys, in adolescence this pattern is reversed and females are more likely than males to suffer from chronic (but not life threatening) illnesses and psychological disturbances (Sweeting 1995). However, while females are more likely to become ill during adolescence, males are more likely to die (Sweeting 1995).

One of the implications of the lack of sociological research into the health of young people has been a tendency to assume that factors which are strongly associated with the distribution of health risks in childhood and adulthood (such as social class) have an equally powerful affect in youth. In fact one of the few sociologists who has focused specifically on the health of young people, Patrick West, has challenged this view. Rather than representing a continuity of patterns evident among younger and older age groups, the West hypothesis maintains that early youth is a period of relative equality (West 1988, forthcoming). Drawing on national statistics such as the British Census, the General Household Surveys and the longitudinal 'West of Scotland Twenty-07 Study', West has analysed the distribution of a number of illnesses and symptoms among young people from different social backgrounds. The conclusion he draws is that although there is a significant correlation between social class and a range of measures of ill-health in childhood and adulthood, early youth is a period of relative equity. After reviewing evidence relating to the social distribution of seven aspects of health (mortality, chronic illness, self-related health, symptoms of acute illness, accidents and injuries, mental health and specific conditions)[1] West argues that severe chronic illness (which is class differentiated from infancy) is the only dimension on which social class can be seen as significantly related to health.

West can be criticized on the grounds that while health inequalities in early adolescence appear to be absent, physical variations and differences in health related behaviours which have implications for health in later life can still be identified among this age group (Bennett and Williams 1994). Macintyre (1988), for example, has argued that the well established correlation between social class and height reflects underlying variations in standards of nutrition and health status which will be reflected in the distribution of degenerative diseases in adult life. It can also be argued that important sources of health variation stem from occupational experiences in adult life which will serve to reinforce class and gender differences in later life.

Aside from noting that females are more likely than males to suffer ill-health in adolescence and that a pronounced class differential in the health of young people appears to be absent, it is not within the scope of this chapter to engage in a detailed discussion of the epidemiology of youth; indeed, as a consequence of the invisibility of youth in the eyes of many medical researchers, there is a lack of trend data which can be drawn on to comment on changes in the distribution of health risks. In the remainder of this chapter we intend to focus first on some specific aspects of young people's health which have been seen as symptomatic of the increased sources of stress which stem from the unpredictable nature of life in high modernity: poor mental health and related increases in suicide, suicidal behaviour and eating disorders. Second, we focus on the social distribution of health related behaviours (such as smoking, use of alcohol and sex) which may have implications for health.

Mental health

Evidence from a number of sources suggests that changing transitional experiences may have resulted in increased levels of stress which are subsequently manifest in psychological ill-health (Smith and Rutter 1995; West and Sweeting 1996). Although youth transitions have always involved some psychological adjustment as young people attempt to establish adult identities, levels of depression and stress related problems among the younger generation appear to have increased. Indeed, it has been argued that since 1945, psycho-social disorders (including depression, eating disorders and suicidal behaviours) among adolescents have become 'substantially more prevalent' (Smith and Rutter 1995), and over the last ten years the numbers of young people diagnosed as mentally ill or admitted to mental hospitals has increased (SCEC 1994). However, this evidence needs to be approached cautiously as people have become more likely to seek professional help for psychological problems and doctors have become more predisposed to diagnosing psychological malaise (Hill 1995).

The risk of depression does increase substantially during the teenage years, especially among young women (Meeus 1994; Smith and Rutter 1995; West and Sweeting 1996). In this context, adolescence has been referred to as a 'window of risk' (Burke *et al.* 1990). In a longitudinal study of 1,000 young people in the west of Scotland, evidence of psychological morbidity was found in around a third of males and two-fifths of females at age 18 (West and Sweeting 1996). These findings are broadly in line with those of a number of other writers. In a comparison of young people in three European countries, Offer and colleagues (1988) reported that nearly three in ten young people (27 per cent) suffer from depression. Moreover, evidence suggests that between 10 and 15 per cent of adolescents have serious emotional or behavioural problems (Kutcher 1994).

The reduction in psychological well-being among young people can be seen as reflected in an increase in suicide and eating disorders. Since the 1950s, the suicide rate among young people has increased, while suicides have declined among older people (Smith and Rutter 1995). In part, these differences reflect the greater acceptability of suicide among the younger generation; according to Hill, 'parents are more likely to judge suicide in religious and moral terms, while their children regard it in terms of individual rights' (1995: 89). It has also been suggested that the media has made young people more familiar with suicide; it has been argued, for example, that in the USA the average young person will have seen around 800 screen suicides prior to leaving school (Hill 1995). Celebrity suicides (real or fictional) have also been linked to fluctuations in the suicide rate (Hill 1995).

Since the mid-1970s, the increase in male suicides has been particularly sharp among 15- to 19-year-olds, although during this period there was little change in the female suicide rate. As a result of these trends, by 1990 male 15- to 19-year-olds were almost four times as likely as females to take their own lives (Woodroffe *et al.* 1993). Yet while the sharp increase in male suicides is a cause for concern, it is important to stress that relatively few young people take their own lives: the annual suicide rate among 16- to 19-year-olds is currently around 6 per 100,000 for males and between 1 and 2 per 100,000 for females (West and Sweeting 1996).

While suicide among young people remains relatively rare, parasuicide and suicidal thoughts are more common.[2] Throughout the 12 to 17 age range (and especially in mid-adolescence), young people become increasingly likely to consider suicide, with females being most likely to consider taking their own lives (Diekstra *et al.* 1995; Smith and Rutter 1995). Males however, are most successful in taking the act through to conclusion, partly because they tend to choose more aggressive methods (Diekstra *et al.* 1995). In a survey of 15,000 Dutch students, Diekstra and colleagues (1991) found that almost one in five (19 per cent) had entertained suicidal thoughts during the past year, although obviously many of those who contemplate suicide subsequently fail to take any action. Statistics on parasuicide vary considerably depending on the source of information and it is argued that only around a quarter of cases are brought to the attention of the medical authorities (Diekstra *et al.* 1995). In a review of literature on parasuicides since 1985, Diekstra and colleagues (1995) argue that in any year, according to the source of statistics used, between 2 and 20 per cent of young people attempt to end their lives. Trends in parasuicide suggest that while rates increased between the 1960s and 1980s, there has been a decline during the last decade (Platt and Kreitman 1990; Diekstra *et al.* 1995).

Another symptom of increased stress in adolescence relates to eating disorders. Eating disorders such as anorexia nervosa and bulimia nervosa are most common in adolescence and early adulthood (Mennell *et al.* 1992; Fombonne 1995; Rutter and Smith 1995). The distribution of anorexia is bi-modal with peaks at around the ages of 14 and 18 (Hsu 1990; Mennell *et al.* 1992; Fombonne 1995) while the average age for the onset of bulimia is between 19 and 20. Both anorexia and bulimia are disorders which tend to be concentrated among white, middle-class, female teenagers. Young women are more likely than young men to develop both of these disorders by a ratio of around ten to one (Fombonne 1995; Smith and Rutter 1995) and they are much more prevalent among those from middle-class families (Jones *et al.* 1980; Hsu 1990). Indeed, Fombonne (1995) argues that obesity carries less of a social stigma among lower class women: peer groups are important in this context and eating disorders are seen as rife in educational institutions. Although members of ethnic minorities are less likely to suffer from eating disorders, among black women the highest rates tend to be found among those from upwardly mobile families (Garfinkel and Garner 1982).

Although eating disorders are more common among middle-class women, females from working-class families are increasingly subject to the same media and peer pressure as they come to spend longer periods in full-time education. Indeed, the fastest growth in anorexia is currently to be found among working-class women (Garfinkel and Garner 1982) and the working classes seem to be following an historical trend whereby slimness becomes adopted as an ideal once a social group acquires the means to indulge their appetite (Mennell *et al.* 1992).

A number of writers have suggested that the age distribution of eating disorders reflect the impact of key transitions. The first peak in the age distribution of anorexia, for example, coincides with the development of sexual maturity and it is argued that the weight changes associated with the onset of puberty lead to bodily dissatisfaction among young women which can trigger eating disorders. Conversely, males tend to regard an increase in body weight as something which enhances their masculinity (Fombonne 1995). The second peak in anorexia coincides with the transition from adolescence to adulthood and may reflect increased pressure to succeed in education and the labour market and to be accepted socially outside of family-based circles (Fombonne 1995).

Although there has been some debate about the extent to which the rising number of recorded cases of anorexia and bulimia represent a real underlying trend rather than a medically fashionable diagnosis, Mennell and colleagues (1992) suggest that the balance of evidence seems to rest in favour of the former argument. Anorexia nervosa was first recognized during the last century, although it has only received serious attention since the 1970s (Mennell *et al.* 1992; Fombonne 1995). In the modern world, it is fashionable to be thin and slimness is associated with positive attributes such as success and sexual attractiveness. Conversely, plumpness is associated with negative traits, such as laziness, and fat people are often portrayed as unhealthy and as sexually repulsive (Mennell *et al.* 1992). Various studies have highlighted the role of the media in promoting the association between positive social attributes and low body weight (Kaufman 1980; Garfinkel and Garner 1982). Kaufman (1980) studied the portrayal of female characters in American television commercials and argued that slim women tended to be portrayed as intelligent, popular and attractive. Highlighting the promotion of unrealistically thin body images, Garfinkel and Garner (1982) argued that although the average weight of women has been increasing, successful models and beauty contest participants have been getting thinner. In a study of Miss America contestants and *Playboy* centrefolds, Garfinkel and Garner (1982) showed that since the 1970s, average weight has declined and that winners of the Miss America contest tend to weigh significantly less than other contenders.

While most young women do not suffer from medically diagnosable forms of anorexia and bulimia, the desire to control weight is central to the lives of many young women. Concern about weight is common among the female population. Button and Whitehouse (1981), for example, suggest that between 80 and 90 per cent of women in the industrialized world monitor their calorie intake and frequently fail to eat enough to satisfy their appetites. Among 16- to 19-year-olds, it has been shown that around one in three have dieted to lose weight (Rudat *et al.* 1992). As Fombonne suggests, ' "normative discontent" with weight is now part of the day to day psychological life of most young women, accompanied, at least temporarily, by some alteration in their behaviour' (1995: 647). Indeed, Mennell and colleagues (1992) argue that many of the symptoms of medically diagnosable disorders exist among a sizeable minority of the female population. Symptoms of bulimia, such as binge eating, are present in more than one in ten of the 18- to 22-year-old population (Meadows *et al.* 1986), while it has been estimated that between 20 and 30 per cent of adolescents are obese (Parry-Jones 1988).

In Giddens's (1991) view, eating disorders are significant as he regards them as a modern phenomenon, linked to the desire to establish a distinct self-identity. As he expresses it, 'anorexia can be understood as a pathology of reflexive self-control, operating around an axis of self-identity and bodily appearance, in which shame anxiety plays a preponderant role' (1991: 104). In this interpretation, eating disorders are seen as a determined attempt to control body image and identity during a period in which young people are increasingly denied autonomy in many other aspects of their lives.

Others have argued that eating disorders are a consequence of the patriarchal organization of society (Minuchin 1978) or rooted in female socialization (Boskind-Lodahl 1976). It has also been suggested that the rise of the feminist movement has been partly responsible for the increase in eating disorders. The role of homeworker and mother have been portrayed as demeaning and women encouraged to pursue success in other, previously male dominated, fields. Chernin, for example, argues that

> the recent epidemic of eating disorders must be understood as a profound development crisis in a generation of women still deeply confused, after twenty years of struggle for female liberation, about what it means to be a woman in the modern world.
>
> (1986: 12, quoted in Mennell *et al.* 1992: 53)

The increased health risks posed by eating disorders, suicidal behaviours and other mental health problems have common causes. To an extent each of these changes arise out of the protraction and desequencing of transitions and from the increased uncertainty with which young people move into the labour market and assume domestic and housing responsibilities. Three potential causes are worthy of further consideration here. First, the lack of jobs, high levels of unemployment and the associated feeling of helplessness among young people may be reflected in mental health problems and suicidal behaviours. Second, the protraction of the school to work transition and, in particular, changing transitional sequences, may mean that young people are forced into making particular transitions before they have accomplished learning tasks associated with previous transitions. The protraction of school to work transitions also leads to an increased significance of the peer group and conformity to group norms and standards which, for young women, can mean conformity to stereotyped body images. Third, increased dependency in the post-adolescent phase, combined with changes in family relations can lead to stressful conflicts and a lack of control over significant life events.

This deterioration in the mental health of young people seems to have been affected by changes in post-16 experiences; young people today face greater uncertainties and it is more common for them to enter situations where their expectations conflict with their subsequent experiences (Furlong 1992). Furlong and Spearman (1989) measured the psychological well-being of a nationally representative sample of young Scots and made comparisons between young people in different situations. Those who were unemployed were found to have the lowest psychological well-being. The link between unemployment and mental health has been highlighted by a number of writers (Fryer and Payne 1986; Warr 1987; West and Sweeting 1996) and it is likely that the uncertainty associated with placement on schemes may also have implications for mental health. Furlong and Spearman (1989) argued that unexpected transitional outcomes had psychological repercussions; young people with above average qualifications who entered low-skill segments of the labour market, for example, tended to suffer in terms of mental health. Moreover, Smith and Rutter (1995) suggest that the rise in expectations associated with lengthening educational experience can have an adverse effect on mental health if they ultimately lead to disappointment.

Expressing concern over the impact of economic restructuring on young people, West and Sweeting argue that the 'economic recession, unemployment, low paid jobs and the sense of having no future are all potentially components of a social malaise that may affect the health of us all, but especially the young' (1996: 50). Psychologists also provide evidence that the incidence of a highly stressful life event, or especially the *accumulation* of stressful events, and a sense of hopelessness are linked to suicidal behaviours (Jacobs 1971; D'Attilio *et al.* 1992; de Wilde *et al.* 1992).

Although there is a large body of literature highlighting a connection between unemployment and mental health problems (Banks and Jackson 1982; Hammer 1992; West and Sweeting 1996), Smith and Rutter (1995) remain sceptical about the extent to which changing levels of aggregate unemployment can be used as predictors of general trends in mental health. Despite low rates of unemployment, psycho-social disorders rose sharply during the 1950s and 1960s. Moreover, they argue that the rapid rise in unemployment during the 1930s and in the recession of the late 1970s and early 1980s was not matched by a corresponding rise in disorders.

While general trends in psychological malaise may be weakly correlated with unemployment rates, there is plenty of evidence suggesting that personal experience of unemployment leads to an increase in mental health problems. Using longitudinal evidence, West and Sweeting (1996) found that among males and females the experience of unemployment was associated with a significant increase in psychological morbidity (General Health Questionnaire 'caseness') compared to members of their sample who did not experience unemployment. They also report that rates of attempted suicide among unemployed youth (9 per cent of males and 7 per cent of females) were much higher than among those in jobs or on schemes. In Edinburgh, Platt and Kreitman (1990) found a strong correlation between fluctuations in unemployment rates and levels of parasuicide. However, Diekstra and colleagues (1995) cast doubt on the causal significance attributed to unemployment by these authors and argued that during the 1970s there was an overall increase in attempted suicide by employed men and a decrease in parasuicide among the unemployed.

While there remains some doubt about the relationship between unemployment and parasuicide within the general population, recent changes in the labour market mean that many young people feel personally vulnerable to unemployment and a number of writers have linked anticipated unemployment with a deterioration in mental health (Kasl *et al.* 1975; West and Sweeting 1996). West and Sweeting (1996) found that in 1987 the possibility of future unemployment was the main concern of 15-year-olds in their Scottish sample. More than eight in ten respondents (82 per cent) reported that they were worried 'a lot' or 'a bit' about becoming unemployed. Those with parents in manual occupations and those expecting to enter the labour market at a relatively early stage tended to be most concerned about the prospect of unemployment. Among 21-year-olds, West and Sweeting (1996) report that more than one in ten (13 per cent) thought it 'very likely' or 'quite likely' that they would become unemployed within five years; among these respondents the risk of psychological morbidity was two and a half times greater than among those who thought they were unlikely to become unemployed.

The greater protraction of the youth transitions, changes in the sequence of key transitions and the prolongation of semi-dependency have also been seen as leading to psycho-social problems. Smith and Rutter (1995), for example, suggest that longer transitions can lead to conflict with parents, particularly as autonomy is granted in a piecemeal fashion. They suggest that smooth transitions are best accomplished one step at a time with young people gaining confidence through the successful completion of one transition before the next is negotiated. However, Smith and Rutter (1995) argue that the increasing malaise among young people is the consequence of a desequencing of transitions rather than protraction *per se*. Indeed, trend data shows that the increase in psycho-social disorders among young people began sometime before transitions began to lengthen.

Furthermore, both Smith and Rutter (1995) and West and Sweeting (1996) suggest that one of the keys to understanding the increasing malaise among young people is the increasing importance of youth cultures. Young people today spend longer periods in the company of their peers and youth cultures have become more isolated from the adult world. Perhaps surprisingly, social class does not seem to be associated with psycho-social problems among young people (Mann *et al.* 1983; Glendinning *et al.* 1992; West forthcoming). Although there are clear class-related gradients associated with the mental health of children and adults, among adolescents social class is not significant (West forthcoming). West argues that these findings can be explained by the cross-cutting effects of the school, peer group and youth culture which serve to reduce the strength of factors associated with social background. Indeed, during adolescence friendship networks have been shown to increase in significance relative to the influence of parents (Meeus 1994). Changing family structures have also been seen as related to increasing psycho-social problems of young people. Although the evidence linking family breakdown with mental health problems is inconclusive (Shafii 1989), the lack of parental support or involvement which may accompany family breakdown appears to have a significant effect (Smith and Rutter 1995). Indeed, it has been suggested that 'between 1960 and 1985 the divorce rates of European countries were among the most accurate predictors of changes in youth suicide' (Hill 1995: 73).

Health related behaviours

While there is some evidence of an increased risk of psycho-social disorders among young people, it is important to stress that the majority move through adolescence and into adulthood with their physical and mental health intact; any conclusions about whether the apparent increase in health problems among this generation of youth will be reflected in their health as adults would be premature given the inconclusive nature of much of the data. Yet while most young people remain healthy, many forms of behaviour which are common among young people do have consequences for long-term health. In this section we focus specifically on the risks which stem from smoking, alcohol consumption, drug use and from sexual encounters and examine the extent to which these risks are unevenly distributed throughout the youth population.

Smoking and drinking

Despite a reduction in smoking among the general population in Britain, which can be traced back to the early 1960s, the decline in the use of tobacco by young people has been less sharp than among the adult population and a significant number of young people will use tobacco during their teenage years (Lader and Matheson 1991; Woodroffe *et al.* 1993). The

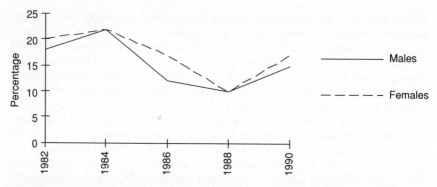

Figure 6.1 Proportion of 11–15-year-olds who smoke regularly or
occasionally: 1982–90
Source: Lader and Matheson 1991

use of tobacco by young people tends to be associated with social class and
educational attainment. Young people from working-class families are marginally more likely to smoke than those from middle-class families (mainly
because of a link between smoking in parents and their children), as are
those who leave school at an early stage (Green *et al.* 1991; Plant and Plant
1992). Prior to the 1980s, males were more likely to smoke than females.
However, the decline in smoking has been sharpest among the male population and by the late 1980s similar proportions of 16–19-year-old males and
females could be classified as regular smokers (28 per cent), with males in
this age group smoking an average of 89 cigarettes per week compared to 80
for young women (Foster *et al.* 1990; Woodroffe *et al.* 1993). Among those
of secondary school age (11–15) in England, 9 per cent of males and 11 per
cent of females smoked regularly in 1990 (Lader and Matheson 1991). Since
the early 1980s, secondary school age females have been more likely than
males to smoke (Figure 6.1). Between 1984 and 1988, there was a decline in
smoking among males and female school children, although from 1988 the
trend was reversed, especially among young women who have been targeted
by tobacco industry advertising campaigns (Lader and Matheson 1991;
Woodroffe *et al.* 1993).

Given the serious risks associated with smoking, the reduction in the
proportion of young people who smoke has long-term consequences for the
health of young people. Indeed, as Plant and Plant note, significantly more
young people are likely to die through diseases linked to tobacco than AIDS
and therefore a decline in smoking is likely to lead to a significant fall in
premature death: 'among 1,000 young adult males in England and Wales
who smoke cigarettes on average about 1 will be murdered, 6 will be killed
on the roads and 250 will be killed before their time by tobacco' (1992: 62).

Like smoking, under-aged drinking is common. Young people in Britain are brought up within a 'wet culture' (Plant and Plant 1992) in which the
introduction to social drinking is an important rite of passage on the road
to adulthood. Balding (1993) shows that only 14 per cent of today's 14- to

15-year-olds will not have tried alcohol, while Fossey and colleagues (1996) suggest that around a third of boys and girls are consuming alcohol regularly by the age of 16. Lister Sharp (1994) argues that by the age of 16 around 90 per cent of young people in Britain will have sampled alcoholic drinks. Parental drinking habits have a significant impact on young people's use of alcohol, with middle-class youth tending to drink more than those from working-class families (Green *et al.* 1991). Among young people between the ages of 9 and 15, slightly more Afro-Caribbeans than whites will have tried alcohol (71 per cent to 61 per cent), while relatively few Asian youths will have tasted alcohol (19 per cent) (HEA 1992).

Between 1970 and 1988 per capita consumption of alcohol increased from 5.3 to 7.4 litres per year (Brewers Society 1990, quoted in Plant and Plant 1992) and the level of alcohol consumption today is twice as high as it was in the mid-1950s (Alcohol Concern 1991). Despite the increased use of alcohol among the general population, there is no evidence that young people's drinking patterns have changed over the last 20 years (Fossey *et al.* 1996). In fact the evidence suggests that for young people the short-term health risks associated with drinking have decreased, partly as a result of drink-driving campaigns. Plant and Plant (1992), for example, show that between 1979 and 1989 there was a sharp reduction (by over 50 per cent) in fatalities among 16–19-year-old drivers associated with high alcohol consumption. However, although drink-related road deaths have declined, the use of alcohol is still frequently associated with car accidents and violent crime and is among the main causes of death among young people (Woodroffe *et al.* 1993; SCEC 1994).

Despite the normality of alcohol use among young people, their drinking patterns frequently cause concern among the adult population and have been the focus of numerous moral panics. In recent years, media attention on the so-called lager louts led to legislation which enabled local authorities to prohibit outdoor drinking in specified public areas. In the west of Scotland, concerns have been expressed over the popularity of fortified wines such as Buckfast which some claim to be associated with violent crimes. At the time of writing, the press have been drawing attention to the 'dangers' of alcoholic lemonades, such as Hooch and Two Dogs, which have been marketed towards younger drinkers. Yet while most young people consume alcoholic beverages, the majority drink relatively small amounts and alcohol dependence and chronic heavy drinking is unusual in under-21-year-olds (Fossey *et al.* 1996). However, Fossey and colleagues show that a 'substantial minority' (1996: 58) of young males and females drink heavily. Among 14- to 16-year-olds in England, for example, around one in ten boys and one in twenty girls claimed to have drunk in excess of 11 units of alcohol in their last drinking session, with corresponding figures for Scotland being almost twice as high for males and females (Plant and Foster 1991; Plant *et al.* 1991).[3] Among 18- to 24-year-olds, it has been shown that around 10 per cent of females and 33 per cent of males exceed the recommended weekly intake of alcohol (Goddard 1991).

Among young people, drinking is associated with sociability and maturity (Davies and Stacey 1972) and there may be considerable social pressure to drink heavily on occasions. Although most young people consume moderate amounts of alcohol, Marsh and colleagues (1986) report that just over half of the males in their sample of 17-year-olds (53 per cent) and less than a third of females (30 per cent) said that they had been drunk at least once. Plant and colleagues (1985) reported that around one in three males in the 15- to 16-year-old age group (31 per cent) and around one in four females (26 per cent) had experienced a hangover. Although the introduction to alcohol forms an important part of normal transitions to adulthood, many of the risks stem from the links between alcohol and anti-social behaviour, such as vandalism, fighting and petty crime (Marsh *et al.* 1986; and see Chapter 7, this volume) as well as through the greater risk of road accidents (as pedestrians as well as drivers), suicide (Hill 1995) and the tendency to engage in unprotected sex (Plant and Plant 1992).

Use of drugs and solvents

Since the 1950s, associations have been made between youth and drug cultures. In the 1960s, drugs like cannabis and LSD were an important part of hippie culture, while in the 1990s use of ecstasy has become common among ravers. Like alcohol, drug use is a normal part of the adolescent experience and there is evidence that young people who use drugs most frequently are the same as those who drink or smoke excessively (Plant 1989). There is also strong evidence to suggest that young people today are more likely to experiment with drugs than they were a decade ago (Measham *et al.* 1994). While many recreational drugs carry no greater risk to the health of the user than alcohol or tobacco, the illegality of many of these substances, combined with frequent media-generated moral panics over usage (especially over new fashion drugs such as ecstasy and ketamine), mean that users risk police attention and legal sanctions (see Chapter 7, this volume).

Among the 14- to 25-year-old population, almost one in two males and one in three females have experimented with drugs (mostly cannabis) (Graham and Bowling 1995), with the majority having had the opportunity to partake or having friends who used drugs. Among the young adolescents, solvents are used fairly widely and there has been a rise in the number of deaths attributed to solvents over the last ten years (Plant and Plant 1992; Rutter and Smith 1995). In a survey of 29,072 young people between the ages of 11 and 16, Balding (1993) showed that the use of drugs and solvents increased from around 3 per cent at age 11 and 12, to 31 per cent between the ages of 15 and 16 (Figure 6.2). Newcombe (1987) found that among 15- to 20-year-olds in areas such as London, Edinburgh and Merseyside the majority were likely to have one or more friends who took drugs. A sizeable minority of today's youth will use soft drugs such as cannabis and ecstasy on a regular basis. Graham and Bowling (1995), for example, show that one in three males and one in five females aged between 14 and 25 use cannabis at least once a week, while among 15- to 16-year-olds, Balding (1993) has shown that 28 per cent of males and 22 per cent of females had used the drug. Although cannabis is the most used drug, the 1992 British Crime Survey shows that

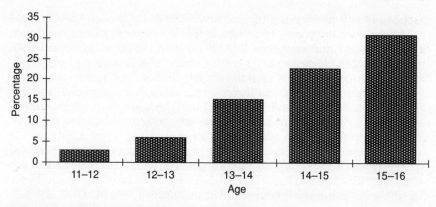

Figure 6.2   Use of illegal drugs and solvents, by age
Source: Balding 1993

almost one in ten 16- to 19-year-olds had tried ecstasy (9 per cent) amphet-
amines (9 per cent) and LSD (8 per cent) (Mott and Mirrless-Black 1993) and
evidence from a number of sources suggests that young people's use of most
of these drugs has increased in recent years (Plant 1989; Mott and Mirrless-
Black 1993; Measham *et al.* 1994).

One popular myth is that drug use is particularly heavy amongst black
youth. Figures relating to self-reported usage suggest that white youths are
more likely to have used drugs than Afro-Caribbeans with Asians having the
lowest level of consumption (Graham and Bowling 1995). However, there is
evidence that the use of heroin and crack tends to be highest among Afro-
Caribbean, Pakistani and Bangladeshi populations (Maung 1995).

While overall levels of drug use are highest among middle-class youth,
those from working-class families appear to be more likely to use 'hard' drugs
and are more likely to take drugs intravenously (Leitner *et al.* 1993). The
majority of known addicts are under the age of 30 (Silbereisen *et al.* 1995).
There is also evidence for an increase in the use of hard drugs, such as heroin
and cocaine among young people, with the number of registered addicts
having doubled over the last decade. Indeed, according to Home Office figures, between 1968 and 1984 the number of known addicts rose from 2,782
to 12,489 and in 1994 there was an increase of 17 per cent (a small decrease
on the previous year) (Stimson 1987). These increases have led to talk of a
'heroin epidemic', yet the proportion of young people who try hard drugs
remains small; a 1992 survey of 15- to 24-year-olds showed that just one in
a hundred had used heroin or cocaine (Gallup/Wrangler 1992). Indeed, Mott
has argued that despite media coverage of 'increasing' use of crack, evidence
for an 'epidemic' has mainly been drawn from statistics relating to high
risk groups or clinic populations. As Fazey argues, 'backgrounds of severe
social deprivation and high unemployment characterise a disproportionate
number of those with severe enough problems to attend drug treatment
clinics' (1991: 23).

Patterns of drug use are affected by opportunities in the form of local

supply and fashions (Young 1971; O'Bryan 1989). On some inner city housing estates hard drugs may be readily available and those without work may
be particularly vulnerable (Haw 1985; Plant *et al.* 1985; Peck and Plant 1986;
Parker *et al.* 1987; Pearson 1987; Pearson *et al.* 1987; Leitner *et al.* 1993). On
one estate in the Wirral, Newcombe (1987) showed that as many as one in
ten unemployed male school-leavers were using heroin or similar drugs.
Similarly, Burr (1989) found that heroin users tended to come from families
affected by adverse circumstances; users were concentrated among the under
25 age group and were predominantly male.

While there is evidence to suggest that the use of heroin has increased,
there have been important changes in patterns of usage. Over the last decade, the price of heroin has fallen (from US$122 per gram in 1983 to US$94
in 1993) while the quality has tended to improve (Farrell *et al.* 1996). In
turn, heroin started to be used by a broader cross-section of the population
(Mott 1991). While heroin use in the 1960s tended to be a rather isolated
activity with users being described as 'bohemian' or 'counter-cultural' (Stimson
1987), today's user is less marginalized and will frequently inhale the drug
(known as 'chasing the dragon') rather than injecting. Indeed, the growing
popularity of heroin has been linked to the trend towards inhalation (Auld
et al. 1986; South 1994) and the concerns expressed about increased heroin
use perhaps reflect the extent to which use is increasing among middle-class
youth (South 1994).

The other major change in the use of heroin relates to the geographical
distribution of users. Whereas in the 1960s users tended to be heavily concentrated in the London area, by the 1980s usage had become common in
all major cities, with particularly large increases in the notification of new
addicts in Merseyside, Glasgow and Edinburgh (Giggs 1991). With the increase
in HIV/AIDS, the rise in heroin usage, combined with its geographical spread,
has frequently caused alarm among politicians and the media (South 1994:
397), even though many new users avoid intravenous methods. The use of
drugs has also been associated with other forms of risk-taking; drug users
often drink heavily, may risk 'unsafe' sex while under the influence of drugs
(Plant and Plant 1992), may become involved in crime (see Chapter 7, this
volume), or attempt suicide (Hill 1995). Indeed, Measham and colleagues
argue that 'drug use is strongly associated with drinking, smoking, early
sexual experience, and various types of deviant and criminal behaviour'
(1994: 289).

Sexual behaviour and sexual diseases

Linked to the process of physiological maturation, sexual experimentation is
central to the experience of youth. Historical evidence suggests that throughout this century there has been a steady growth in the proportion of young
people who engage in premarital sex (Humphries 1991; Breakwell 1992). In
Britain today, around half of 16-year-old males and females will have had
sexual intercourse, a figure which increases to about 85 per cent by the age
of 20 (Breakwell 1992), while among the 16 to 20 age group two-thirds of

males and more than seven in ten females will have engaged in active and passive oral sex (Breakwell 1992). Despite the availability of contraceptives, one of the main health risks associated with teenage sex is still unwanted pregnancy (which in the 1950s and 1960s carried greater social stigma and was often swiftly followed by increased responsibility as teenage pregnancy tended to be followed by an early marriage). Recent figures show that almost one in ten females in Scotland have had a pregnancy terminated by the age of 20 (Scottish Health Service 1996). Although young people may be aware of the importance of taking precautions, teenage sex often occurs under the influence of alcohol and research shows that young men who consume alcohol prior to sexual intercourse are three times less likely to use condoms (Plant and Plant 1992).

While young people have always had to contend with the risk of contracting sexually transmitted diseases, over the last twenty years there has been a decline in the incidence of treatable infections, such as gonorrhoea and syphilis, but an increase in the potentially life threatening HIV infections, especially since the late 1980s (Plant and Plant 1992). Indeed, with an effective cure for gonorrhoea and syphilis only becoming available in the 1940s, it can be argued that aside from the short period between the 1950s and 1970s sexual activity among young people has tended to involve risks.

Although young people are tending to have intercourse at an earlier age than previously (Foreman and Chilvers 1989; Breakwell 1992), it is important not to portray them as promiscuous; research has shown that the majority of young people have two or fewer sexual partners (Johnson *et al.* 1989) and there is little evidence that young people today are experiencing a greater number of sexual partners (Breakwell 1992). In a recent study of 16-year-olds, just over six in ten (63 per cent) sexually active young men reported having just the one sexual partner during the previous year, compared to nearly eight in ten young women (79 per cent) (Durex 1990, quoted in Plant and Plant 1992). However, many sexual relationships are casual; in a study of young people in Glasgow, for example, half of the sample reported a sexual relationship in which intercourse had taken place on just one occasion (Wight 1993). While numbers of sexual partners show little variation by social class (Foreman and Chilvers 1989), there is evidence that those living in deprived neighbourhoods tend to have their first sexual encounters at an earlier age (O'Reilly and Aral 1985) and are less likely to use condoms (Bagnall and Plant 1991). On the other hand, those in the highest attainment bands tend to be slightly older when they first have intercourse, and are marginally more likely to use condoms (Breakwell 1992). In this context, sexual activity can be seen as posing a greater health risk for lower working-class youths who are more likely to become pregnant while teenagers and are more vulnerable to sexual disease.

The sharp increase in the incidence of HIV and deaths from AIDS, government sponsored campaigns and the publicity generated by AIDS related celebrity deaths have all helped encourage condom use (Selzer *et al.* 1989; Sonenstein *et al.* 1989). However, many teenagers who have multiple partners continue to have unprotected sex and it has been argued that 'most young people do not at present use condoms and few use them routinely' (Plant and Plant 1992: 102). Indeed, Plant and Plant (1992) suggest that coverage of HIV/AIDS by the media has often left young people with the impression that heterosexuals are relatively safe from infection. In a study of 908 18-year-olds in Glasgow, nearly half of the males and a third of the females admitted using no contraceptives at first intercourse (West *et al.* 1993).

In recent years relationships with same sex partners have become more socially acceptable, especially among the younger generation (as reflected in a lowering of the age of consent for homosexual sex to 18 in the Criminal Justice Act of 1994, the inclusion of homosexual characters in popular television soap operas and the scheduling of 'Gaytime TV'). While practising homosexuals appear to have a higher risk of contracting HIV, the numbers of young people who experiment with homosexual intercourse has remained small. In a study of 16- to 21-year-olds, just 2 per cent of the sample defined their sexuality as either homosexual or bisexual (Ford and Morgan 1989). Similarly, Foreman and Chilvers (1989) found that just less than 2 per cent of males reported experience of homosexual intercourse. A 1970 study by the Kinsey Institute (Fay *et al.* 1989) puts the figure slightly higher, with around 4 per cent of males reporting experience of homosexual intercourse and just less than 2 per cent having regular or occasional homosexual relationships. While self-reported figures for homosexual activity remain low, heterosexual anal intercourse has been identified as a potential source of HIV risk, an experience reported by more than one in ten (11 per cent) male and female 16- to 20-year-olds (Breakwell 1992).

Conclusion

In this chapter we have highlighted some of the health risks faced by young people and described changes in forms of behaviour which may pose threats to their health. In terms of general health, with the absence of reliable trend data it is difficult for us to speculate about whether there has been a weakening in traditional sources of inequality. It is likely that adolescence has always been a period in which the major health inequalities lie dormant and that the differential experiences of young people are reflected in the re-emergence of inequalities based on class and gender as an age cohort moves into adulthood. On the other hand, it is possible that we are witnessing significant changes. Class and gender differences in many health related behaviours are relatively small and this may lead to a process of equalization in adulthood. Although some forms of risky behaviour are more common among working-class youth (such as smoking), other risky activities are more prevalent among the middle classes (such as use of alcohol and soft drugs). Similarly, males and females are vulnerable in different ways, but on balance the differences are not striking.

While relatively few young people have to cope with difficulties stemming from diseases or poor physical health during adolescence, there is evidence that the social conditions of high modernity are reflected in a deterioration in mental health which are manifest in different ways among males and females. Depression, eating disorders, suicide and attempted suicide have all become more common and can be seen as reflecting the increased incidence of 'fateful moments' (Giddens 1991) and the ongoing sense of doubt which is a central feature of high modernity and which can be particularly threatening for young people in the process of establishing adult identities. To an extent, these risks have an impact on the lives of all young people, although clearly some are particularly vulnerable to the health risks which stem from labour market marginalization or exclusion. On balance, the evidence on the changing health of young people lends some support for the ideas of Beck and Giddens in so far as the key changes seem to relate to an increase in psychological problems which can be linked to a heightened sense of insecurity in late modernity.

Notes

1 Specific conditions included cerebral palsy, cystic fibrosis, respiratory problems, ear infections, hearing and visual impairment.
2 The term parasuicide was coined by Kreitman (1977) to refer to suicidal behaviour with a non-fatal outcome. The term is used in preference to attempted suicide as intention is treated as problematic. Diekstra and colleagues (1995) argue that motives can be difficult to determine as the majority of young people who come close to dying by their own hand will subsequently deny intention.
3 A unit is the equivalent of half a pint of beer or one glass of wine.

7 Crime *and* insecurity

If it is true that young people grow out of crime, then many will fail
to do so, at least by their mid-twenties, simply because they have not
been able to grow up, let alone grow out of crime.

(Graham and Bowling 1995: 56)

Introduction

In the previous chapter we considered the extent to which recent social
changes have been associated with increased health risks among young people.
In this chapter we focus on crime, which represents a different set of risks.
Reports of crime epidemics frequently make the headlines of newspapers and
many press reports highlight the involvement of young people, often drawing
parallels between an apparent rise in criminal activity and a breakdown in
the social fabric of society. In this chapter we attempt to put some of these
changes into perspective and examine the implications of processes of social
change for young people's involvement in crime. We argue that the sorts of
changes which have occurred do not provide support for the idea that there
has been a breakdown in traditional social values and suggest that changing
patterns of crime are an inevitable consequence of the extension of youth as
a phase in the life cycle. In the context of our discussion about differential
patterns of vulnerability in late modernity, we argue that the risks associated
with illegal activities continue to be unequally distributed according to traditional social divisions such as class and gender. However, this is not to
suggest that there are significant differences in patterns of offending between
social groups, rather that differential risks largely reflect the activities of law
enforcement agencies.

While Durkheim (1964) regarded increasing crime rates as an entirely
normal by-product of social development, some the key characteristics of
late modernity, such as reflexivity of the self and the weakening of collective
identities, are processes which might be seen as undermining the normative
order. Indeed, Merton (1969) highlighted the apparent contradiction between
social norms which place an emphasis on individual achievement and success
on the one hand, and the maintenance of differential opportunity structures
on the other. In this respect, processes of individualization and subjective disembedding, which Beck and Giddens regard as characteristic of late modernity,
could be seen as creating the conditions in which crime is likely to rise.

As those without work or domestic responsibilities are more likely to
be involved in criminal activities (Rutherford 1992), it can be argued that

changing transitional patterns have affected the risk of criminal involvement. Being denied access to the financial rewards of working life and forced into greater dependency on their families, young people may become involved in crime as a way to gain access to consumer culture or simply as part of the quest for excitement or kicks that has long been central to the lives of young people. With a lack of commitments, risk-taking and experimentation are considered to be a normal part of adolescent development. Indeed, it has been argued that risk-taking and the search for adventure 'help adolescents achieve independence, identity and maturity' (Jack 1989: 337). With a decline in manufacturing employment and as a consequence of a lack of opportunities in the youth labour market, the involvement of young males in crime has also been interpreted as an attempt to establish masculine identities in a rapidly changing social world (Campbell 1993; Newburn and Stanko 1994).

While young people frequently engage in activities which shock or provoke reactions among the adult population, such as drug taking or street violence, in late modernity the weakening of communal ties can be seen as leading to feelings of mistrust and insecurity which can lead to an intensification of generational conflict. In this context it can be argued that while the evidence for a significant rise in youth crime is inconclusive, adults and the criminal justice agencies have become preoccupied with crime prevention (Taylor 1996) and suspicious of young people who are perceived as being more lawless than their own generation (Pearson 1994). In turn, young people also feel vulnerable and express concern about becoming the victims of violent crime on the streets and in pubs and clubs.

The 'problem' of crime

Concern about the criminal activities of the young is not a modern phenomenon; Pearson (1994) suggests that politicians and members of the older generation have always tended to regard levels of criminality among the younger generation as abnormal. Whereas adults tend to think of their own generation as orderly and disciplined, standards of behaviour are constantly perceived as having deteriorated. Pearson argues that youth crime has often been regarded as a consequence

> of recent social changes, involving a pattern of complaint linking youthful crime to the 'permissive society'; the break-up of the family and community; the dwindling power of parents, teachers, magistrates, and policemen; the lack of respect among the young for authority in all its forms; and the incitements of demoralizing popular entertainments such as television violence and video nasties which lead to imitative 'copy-cat' crime.
>
> (1994: 1163)

Over the last decade, concerns such as these, together with a perception that juvenile crime is a growing problem, have had an impact on criminal justice policy. In particular, the Conservative government have made political mileage out of the claim that they could deal effectively with the problem of

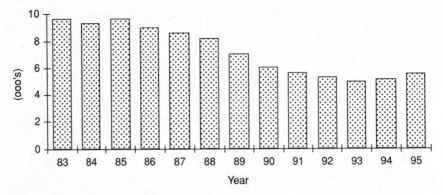

Figure 7.1 Young offenders as sentenced prisoners: 1983–95
Source: Home Office 1996

youth crime through the introduction of harsher sentences and closer surveillance of those given non-custodial punishments. Measures have included
greater use of imprisonment, the 'short, sharp shock', involving short sentences in institutions run along the lines of military boot camps, legislation
requiring courts to use financial penalties against the parents of young offenders, as well as experiments involving the electronic tagging of offenders
to enforce curfews and restrict movement.[1] Yet contrary to the political
rhetoric of the Thatcher administration, there was a steady decline in the
numbers of young people imprisoned throughout the 1980s (Hagell and
Newburn 1994). Over the last few years the situation has changed and the
use of custodial sentences for young people is on the increase, with the
government being committed to providing additional prison accommodation (Figure 7.1). Between 1992 and 1994, for example, the number of 15-
to 21-year-olds in prison increased from 6,783 to 8,610; the number of
15-year-old males receiving custodial sentences increased from 436 in 1990
to 709 in 1994, while the number of 15-year-old females in prison increased
from 11 to 31 (Howard League 1995). Indeed, aside from Turkey, a higher
proportion of young people in England and Wales receive custodial sentences than in any other European country (Howard League 1995).

In recent years there have been a number of events which have been
used by the media as evidence of a rise in the incidence of crime among
young people. During the 1980s and early 1990s the inner city riots were used
to turn the spotlight on young males and to suggest that law and order had
broken down. Disorders in Toxteth, Cardiff and Tyneside, for example, were
characterized by confrontations between young men and the police. Other
significant events which have been used to support this position include the
fatal stabbing of a policeman in October 1985 on Broadwater Farm estate in
London, the abduction and murder of a toddler, James Bulger, in February
1993 by two ten-year-old boys and the killing of a headteacher who intervened
when he witnessed one of his pupils being attacked outside of his school in
December 1995. While it is always possible to find examples of serious crime
committed by young people, the evidence for a rising crime rate is somewhat

contradictory and can reflect the different agendas of those responsible for compiling statistics (Coles 1995).

Criminologists tend to treat official statistics with caution and often challenge the reliability of the underlying trends. In particular, they suggest that criminal statistics may reflect patterns of policing rather than patterns of offending and therefore exaggerate the relative criminality of groups of people who have traditionally been the focus of police surveillance (Muncie and McLaughlin 1995; Coleman and Moynihan 1996). Some observed crimes are frequently not reported to the police (such as street violence), while others remain undetected (especially white collar crimes such as fraud) or are not recorded by the police (such as domestic violence). Although there are difficulties in estimating the relationship between reported and unreported crimes (Pearson 1983), the British Crime Survey shows that just over half of all offences go unreported (CSO 1996), although there are significant differences according to the type of offence. In 1993, for example, it was suggested that of all burglaries in England and Wales, 69 per cent were reported to the police, but just 41 per cent were recorded and ultimately convictions were secured in relation to just 2 per cent of the total (CSO 1996). Moreover, in comparison to many crimes, a high proportion of burglaries are reported (with the growth in reported burglaries partly reflecting an increase in the number of people covered by house contents insurance). Much lower levels of reporting and recording occur, for example, in relation to sex crimes.

Local variations in patterns of reported crime can also reflect differences in the enforcement priorities of local police forces and the recording practices which they adopt (Smith 1995). Although there are significant geographical differentials in levels of crime, with a concentration of police resources in some inner city areas, working-class youths face a greater risk of arrest than middle-class youths who may engage in similar activities in suburban areas with a lower level of policing. In particular, it has been argued that the police are overzealous when it comes to apprehending black males and that poor relations between the police and young blacks has been a key factor in explaining riots in Toxteth, Bradford, Handsworth and Brixton (Scarman 1981; Waller 1981; Schostak 1983).

Due to inconsistencies between areas and changing policies relating to prosecutions which affect official statistics, data from victim surveys or self-report studies are often used to provide a more accurate picture of the prevalence of crime. However, while acknowledging that official statistics may provide a distorted picture of levels of involvement among different groups of people, Lea and Young (1993) suggest that in terms of trends, there is actually a close correlation between official statistics and survey data. Both official statistics and surveys indicate a rise in crime which can be traced back to the early 1950s, although there is evidence of a decline since 1992 (CSO 1996).

Although a high proportion of recorded offences are committed by young people, official statistics for England and Wales show that between 1980 and 1990 the proportion of young people convicted of an offence or cautioned fell by 37 per cent (Hagell and Newburn 1994). With overall levels of recorded crime increasing throughout the 1980s and with concerns being expressed by the police about increased delinquency among young people, these figures provoked controversy. In evidence to the Home Affairs Committee, the Shadow Home Secretary, for example, argued that it was 'difficult to believe Home Office claims that offending by young people had actually gone down across the country' (quoted in Hagell and Newburn 1994: 21). Moreover, the Association of Chief Police Officers argued that with an increase in crime and falling rates of detection during the 1980s, alongside a demographic fall in the numbers of young people, these statistics actually indicated a 54 per cent *increase* in youth crime (Hagell and Newburn 1994). The other significant factor which affects official trends in youth crime relates to the increasing use of informal cautions by the police which was encouraged by the Home Office as a means of reducing prosecutions of young people (Hagell and Newburn 1994).[2] Official statistics show that between 1981 and 1991 the rate of convictions and cautions for indictable offences declined among 10- to 13-year-olds and 14- to 17-year-olds, while increasing among 18- to 20-year-olds (Figure 7.2) (CSO 1995b). These changes are perhaps a consequence of the increased use of informal warnings by the police when dealing with young offenders.

Involvement in crime

Involvement in criminal activities is a normal part of adolescence, Home Office (1993b) figures show that by their mid-30s, more than a third of males will have a conviction. Others will have escaped with a caution, will have evaded arrest or have committed crimes which have not been brought to the attention of the police. Among males and females who have been convicted

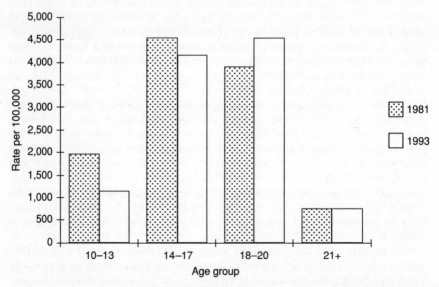

Figure 7.2   Convictions and cautions for indictable offences: 1981–93
Source: CSO 1995b

Table 7.1 Convictions and cautions for indictable offences, by type of offence, gender and age group: 1993

	Males		Females	
	14–17	*18–20*	*14–17*	*18–20*
Theft and handling of stolen goods	47	36	72	62
Other indictable offences	6	15	4	14
Drug offences	10	22	4	11
Violence against the person	13	10	14	9
Burglary	17	13	3	2
Criminal damage	4	3	2	1
Sexual offences	1	1	0	0
Robbery	2	1	1	0

Source: CSO 1996

or cautioned for an offence, the majority have been involved in theft, burglary and the handling of stolen goods (CSO 1996). Few females are convicted or cautioned for burglary, yet similar proportions of both sexes are convicted for involvement in violent crimes (Table 7.1).

Using self-report data from a nationally representative study of 14- to 25-year-olds in England and Wales, Graham and Bowling (1995) describe patterns of participation in a range of criminal activities by young people: more than one in five young males admitted having handled stolen goods, shoplifting, participation in group fighting or disorder in a public place while more than one in ten had been involved in vandalism or theft from work. Females admitted to fewer offences, but more than one in ten had been involved in shoplifting or had handled stolen goods. Both the official statistics and the self-report figures show that involvement in serious crime and persistent offending are relatively rare (Hagell and Newburn 1994; Graham and Bowling 1995; CSO 1996).

Drug offences among young people are relatively common (see Chapter 6), and during the last decade the use of drugs seems to have increased (Measham *et al.* 1994). The number of drug seizures by the police have increased rapidly; by 23 per cent between 1993 and 1994 (the highest ever yearly increase), and more young people are being brought before the courts for possession of controlled drugs (Home Office 1995). However, due to the prevalence of drug use, many young people are now cautioned by the police (particularly for first offences) rather than being brought before the courts. In England and Wales, the proportion of offenders who were cautioned for drug offences rose from 8 per cent in 1984 to 50 per cent in 1992 (Home Office 1995). However, use of hard drugs may be associated with an increased likelihood of involvement in other forms of illegal behaviour. In particular, rises in property related crimes are frequently associated with increased use of heroin. Parker and colleagues (1988), for example, argued that an increase in burglaries in the Wirral on Merseyside was correlated with an increase in heroin use in disadvantaged areas among unemployed youth. In a study of burglary on the Wirral, Parker and Newcombe (1987) found that 50 per cent of offenders were known heroin users.

While under the influence of drugs, users may be less aware of the consequences of their activities (Lyon 1996) and habitual drug use may provide the motivation to commit crimes in order to finance an addiction. Yet Hammersley and colleagues argue that although the use of opiates increased the likelihood of criminal behaviour they 'did not simply and directly cause crime or substantially create criminals from honest citizens' (1990: 19). They concluded that the price of heroin was more related to crime than the addictiveness.

In 1993, young people aged 14 to 25 accounted for 60 per cent of all indictable offences (Home Office 1993c), with a large proportion of those convicted being young black males (Farrington 1990). Young people from working-class families are more likely to be convicted for an offence, with offenders often living in areas of multiple deprivation, having parents who are divorced and with a history of truancy from school (Farrington 1990). Yet while official statistics on convictions highlight an association between social class and criminality, these claims have not been supported by survey data (Graham and Bowling 1995; Hagan *et al.* 1996). Similarly, the strong differences between male and female involvement in crime indicated by official figures have been challenged by survey data (Campbell 1981; Graham and Bowling 1995; Hagan *et al.* 1996). Using self-report data, Graham and Bowling (1995) show that among 14- to 17-year-olds, males and females report similar levels of involvement in offences relating to property and violence (although among older age groups, males reported greater levels of criminal activity). These discrepancies provide support for the view that differential conviction rates reflect patterns of law enforcement rather than underlying gender differences in behaviour.

The higher rates of conviction, prosecution and imprisonment among Afro-Caribbean youth have also been regarded as a reflection of police activity rather than representing greater involvement in crime. Afro-Caribbeans frequently live in inner city areas and tend to be subject to higher levels of police surveillance (Fitzgerald 1993). A report by the Royal Commission on Criminal Justice (Fitzgerald 1993) highlighted a number of factors which were associated with higher levels of conviction and imprisonment among the black population. These included the younger average age of the black population in comparison to that of the white population, the concentration of young blacks in working-class families, lower levels of educational attainment, higher levels of unemployment and their geographical distribution. Moreover, a number of legal factors were also identified which increased their chances of conviction and the severity of the sentence; these included a tendency not to admit guilt (making them ineligible for cautioning and provoking longer sentences if found guilty), the seriousness of offences, the number of previous convictions and the greater tendency for magistrates to refer cases involving black youths to the Crown Court.

While there may be a tendency to exaggerate increases in criminality among the younger generation, there is some evidence that an extension of youth as a stage in the life cycle is likely to lead to a prolonged involvement in crime (Rutherford 1992; Graham and Bowling 1995). However, as yet we are unable to determine whether longer involvement in crime tends to lead to more serious offences. Criminologists have shown that young people's involvement in illegal activities tend to decline as they acquire greater respons- ibilities in work and domestic environments. However, there is also evidence that ageing is associated with a switch from visible crimes committed on the streets (such as violence and car crime) to less visible crime (such as burglary and fraud) (Graham and Bowling 1995). In other words, the lower rates of crime among older youth partly represents higher rates of apprehension and conviction associated with certain types of juvenile crime rather than the termination of involvement.

Older youths and those with domestic or employment responsibilities are less likely to engage in criminal activities than younger people or those with jobs or family responsibilities (Rutherford 1992). Indeed, there is evid- ence that commitment to a job or to another person are associated with a reduction in offending (Parker 1974; Shover 1985; Sampson and Laub 1993). Consequently delays in making key transitions are likely to be reflected in increased levels of criminality. Indeed, young people tend to become less involved in criminal activities as they find ways of gaining fulfilment in other areas of their lives and take on responsibilities in a work or domestic sphere. In particular, relationships with girlfriends have been seen as significant in reducing risk-taking by males (Foster 1990; Coles 1995; Graham and Bowling 1995). However, it has been suggested that with males now facing greater dif- ficulties in the labour market, young women may be less inclined to form steady relationships with young men without obvious prospects (Wallace 1987; Hill 1995). The greater protraction of school to work, domestic and housing transitions for young males is likely to be one of the explanations for the widening gender ratios in offending among the 18 plus age group (Graham and Bowling 1995). In this respect failure to complete a key transition can lead to social marginality and a continuity of the risks associated with criminality.

In this context, transitional experiences are closely related to patterns of involvement in crime and associated with gender differences. Using a multivariate analysis, Graham and Bowling (1995) show that the successful completion of school to work, domestic and housing transitions was associ- ated with an abrupt and conscious end to offending among females. Males, on the other hand, tended to drift away from crime much more gradually and remained susceptible to peer group pressure for sometime after making key transitions. Youth unemployment has also been linked to criminal behaviour; in a longitudinal study of 411 8- to 18-year-olds in London, Farrington and colleagues (1986) reported an increased involvement in criminal activities during periods of unemployment. However, there is evidence that those who are involved in crime prior to entering the labour market experience difficulties in finding jobs. In these circumstances it has been suggested that unemployment is associated with an intensification and prolongation of crim- inal careers (Hagan *et al.* 1996). While there is some evidence to support the theory that unemployment is associated with increased criminal activity, the association has been explained in a number of different ways (Tarling 1982; Hagan *et al.* 1996). On the one hand, it has been argued that an increasing crime rate reflects the collapse of legitimate opportunity structures, on the other, the 'left realists' associate crime with relative deprivation. Lea and Young (1993), for example, argue that crime rises as a consequence of the discontent and frustration which is the inevitable consequence of economic marginalization.

A number of writers have also linked male criminality to difficulties in establishing masculine identities in a changing economic context. With a growth in educational participation, Messerschmidt (1994) argues that males who fail to excel academically frequently see schooling as frustrating their masculinity. Moreover, the decline in manual employment opportunities means that young males today are forced to define their masculinities in new ways with crime offering one route through which positive identities can be established.

Criminal careers

Young people tend to commit their first offences at a relatively young age with a recent survey suggesting that the average age at which males and females start to offend is 13.5 (Graham and Bowling 1995). Those who become involved in car crime, for example, frequently commit their first offence at the age of 13 or 14 (Nee 1993), usually in the company of older peers. In this context, criminologists have argued that patterns of association are particularly significant and that young people become involved in criminal activities in small group settings as they adapt to the norms of peer cultures (Sutherland 1949). Sutherland suggests that individuals engage in criminal acts when such activities are defined as acceptable by their associates. Although Sutherland's theory of differential association has frequently been criticized for suggesting that criminal behaviour is learned (Shoemaker 1990), there is strong evidence that peers have a significant effect on patterns of involvement in crime (Graham and Bowling 1995).

From a different theoretical perspective, Gottfredson and Hirschi (1990) also argue that the amount of time young people spend in the company of their peers has an impact on criminality, with those whose family ties are 'chaotic' tending to spend the greatest amount of time with their friends. Similarly, using self-report data from Northern Ireland, McQuoid suggests that

> juvenile delinquency here is associated with males in their late teens from lower educational and socio-economic groups, who either dislike or who have left school and have no job, have a large circle of 'close' friends, little parental supervision and who do not see the importance of working hard.
>
> (1996: 98)

Control theorists, such as Gottfredson and Hirschi (1990) argue that peer group influence and the lack of close parental supervision provide young people with opportunities to engage in illegal activities either for excitement or financial gain. But opportunities to engage in criminal behaviour are also shaped by the possibilities afforded within a neighbourhood context. Parker (1974), for example, described the ways in which young people living in an inner city area of Liverpool were provided with opportunities for theft in the form of a plentiful supply of cars left by shoppers and city workers. Moreover, young people were easily able to sell stolen car radios due to the existence of a network of 'fences' within the area. The existence of high crime rates in some neighbourhoods has also been seen as reflecting conformity to cultural norms rather than a rejection of accepted patterns of behaviour (Mays 1954; Downes 1966). However, subcultural theories are frequently portrayed as incomplete explanations. Brownfield (1996), for example, argues that the demise of subcultural theories stems from a failure to conceptualize structural and cultural factors within a single explanatory framework.

Street life - gangs

Criminologists have also highlighted the link between criminal activities and blocked access to legitimate opportunities. In settings where legitimate opportunities are restricted, illegal opportunities may arise which help channel young people into delinquency. Young people who are unable to find jobs may find that crime provides them with access to consumer goods and leisure lifestyles which they would otherwise be unable to afford. Referring to the Liverpool 'boys' described by Parker (1974), Pearson argues that the lucrative sale of car radios allowed the boys 'to enjoy the "good times" before either settling down to marriage and family life, or going to prison' (1994: 1180). More recently, Hobbs (1989) has described the ways in which young people in the East End of London develop an entrepreneurial approach to crime aided by family and neighbourhood-based social networks. Similarly, Pryce (1979) described how, for Afro-Caribbean males in Bristol, 'hustling' was used as a means to overcome frustrations caused by the lack of legitimate opportunities (Pearson 1994). In his report on the Brixton disorders, Lord Scarman (1981) drew attention to the ways in which young blacks shared the material expectations encouraged within advanced capitalism, yet as a result of racism and high rates of unemployment often experienced status frustrations. These explanations underline Merton's (1969) arguments about the gap between social norms and aspirations and differential access to opportunities as well as the views of the 'left realists' regarding the consequences of relative deprivation.

Although the association between relative deprivation and crime has merit, it is important to stress that young criminals are often opportunists and frequently lack a profit motive. Many young people become involved in criminal activities as a consequence of seeking new ways of relieving boredom; financial incentives are often of little importance (Nee 1993). Coles, for example, argues that

> early youth crime is often spontaneous, unskilled, committed by a peer group having a bit of a laugh together, and acted out as a piece of hooliganism rather than as a piece of calculated or instrumental rationality.
>
> (1995: 185)

Surely boredom is a result of deprivation?

Young people as victims of crime

While there is evidence that a substantial proportion of crimes are committed by young people, it is also important to stress that young people are frequently the victims of crime and express concerns about perceived personal risks of crime. Much of the research on youth and crime has focused on young people as perpetrators of crime; relatively few writers have explored the implications of fear of crime among the young or analysed the extent to which they are the victims of police harassment or of crimes committed by adults and other young people. Given that a high proportion of criminal acts are committed against young people, this represents a serious bias.

In a study of 250 11- to 15-year-olds in contrasting areas of Edinburgh, Anderson and colleagues (1994) showed that more than four in ten young people worry a lot about the prospect of being attacked by strangers. Indeed, the fear of attack was a particular concern of females with almost six in ten young women being very worried about the possibility of being attacked. Using evidence from the 1992 British Crime Survey, Maung (1995) found that the possibility of sexual pestering or assault by a stranger were the chief concerns of female 12- to 15-year-olds; 56 per cent said that they were very worried about the chances of sexual pestering while 48 per cent were very worried about assault by a stranger. A number also expressed concerns about mugging or burglary (35 per cent and 22 per cent respectively). Boys in the same age range were somewhat less concerned about the possibility of crime; 31 per cent were very worried about sexual pestering, 28 per cent about assault by a stranger, 24 per cent about mugging and 15 per cent about burglary. For each of these crimes, Afro-Caribbean and Asian youth were significantly more likely to express concern about becoming a victim, as were those living in urban areas and areas in which levels of recorded crime were high. These concerns affected the ways in which young people spent their time and the places they visited. In particular, young women are much more likely than young men to feel unsafe when out alone and often felt the need to take precautions against crime, such as making special transport arrangements or going out with friends (Hough 1995).

While fears of crime are not necessarily related to the chances of victimization, young people's behaviour may be affected by the fear of crime. Young people may avoid visiting places they perceive as risky, or may defend themselves against possible attack. In a recent study of 13,432 11- to 16-year-olds in England, more than one in five (22 per cent) admitted carrying offensive weapons on occasions, while among 15 year old boys almost a third had carried a weapon (Carvel 1996). These figures are in line with those reported by other researchers: among 11–15-year-olds in Edinburgh, 30 per cent admitted to carrying knives or other weapons on at least one occasion over a nine month period (Anderson *et al.* 1994) while 34 per cent of young people in Glasgow admitted to carrying knives (Hartless *et al.* 1995).

Studies of young people's experiences of crime show that many of their fears are well founded. Half of the 11- to 15-year-olds interviewed by Anderson and colleagues (1994) had been victims of a crime. Leaving aside offences committed at school or at home, 37 per cent had been assaulted during the previous nine months, 31 per cent had been threatened with violence while 17 per cent had had something stolen. In cases where the offender could be identified, less than half were under the age of 16; 10 per cent of offences against boys and 17 per cent of offences against girls were committed by people over the age of 21 (Anderson *et al.* 1994). Indeed, two-thirds of the girls reported having been harassed by adults, sometimes being followed by people either in cars or on foot.

Again figures from the British Crime Survey are similar in a number of respects. Six out of ten 12- to 15-year-olds had been victims of an incident over the previous six to eight months, a third reported having been assaulted, a fifth had had something stolen and a fifth had been harassed (Maung 1995). Males were significantly more likely than females to have been victims of violent crimes (CSO 1996). Offenders were usually of a similar age and of the same sex as the victim, although older girls (14- and 15-year-olds) frequently reported being assaulted or harassed by older males (Maung 1995).

While crimes committed against young people are a common occurrence, few incidents are reported to the police. Whereas more than a third of adults will tend to report offences such as assaults, robberies, personal threats and thefts, among 16- to 19-year-olds just 14 per cent would make a formal complaint (Maung 1995). Similarly, Anderson and colleagues (1994) showed that 14 per cent of 11- to 15-year-olds would report an assault to the police. Asian and Afro-Caribbean youths are less likely than white youths to report crimes committed against them, although Maung (1995) argues that ethnic differences are not significant once characteristics of areas are taken into consideration. While young people are hesitant about reporting offences to the police, they frequently tell their friends and, depending on the nature of the offence, are likely to bring the matter to the attention of their parents (Anderson *et al.* 1994; Maung 1995). However, females experiencing sexual harassment are frequently unwilling to discuss events with their parents and child abuse is sometimes regarded as an invisible crime.

In many respects, the concentration on young people as the perpetrators of crimes has left us blind to the extent to which young people are victims; they frequently have crimes committed against them and their fears have an impact on their day to day behaviour. In particular, young women frequently experience harassment which they are reluctant to report and which restricts their freedom to go out alone. Moreover, while adults express concerns about 'lawless' youth, many crimes are also committed against young people by adults.

Conclusion

Although many young people engage in criminal activities and while significant numbers will be the victims of crime, it would be wrong to suggest that the patterns of criminality which we have described in this chapter represent a breakdown in the social fabric of society. Young people have always indulged in risky behaviour and in activities which are illegal. The youth of previous generations engaged in similar types of activities and also found themselves to be the focus of police attention (Pearson 1983). There is, however, some evidence that the numbers of crimes committed by young people are rising and that criminal careers are becoming longer. However, the increased teenage crime rate is a reflection of an overall rise in crime and there is no evidence to suggest that the trend in youth crime is anomalous.

In many respects, the problem of crime today relates more to its amplification by the media than to actual risk. Indeed, Hough has suggested that by the 1980s, 'the fear of crime was running ahead of substantive crime problems' (1995: 4). The media focus on abnormal youth crimes has perhaps led to an increased perception of a lawless younger generation and to calls for tougher sanctions against offenders. However, the increased fear of crime has implications for everyone; as Box and colleagues (1988) suggest, the fear of crime can fracture communities as people move away from the cities and restrict their movements. In this context, Giddens (1991) is wrong to suggest that place loses its significance in the age of high modernity; the fear of crime, the chances of becoming a victim of crime and the risks of apprehension for involvement in crime continue to reflect social geographies. While Giddens would argue that through the mass media we are all exposed to the consequences of crime and develop a heightened sense of insecurity and mistrust, perceptions of risk are differentially distributed. Viewers contextualize television violence and are more concerned when the risks highlighted by the media are shown to affect their own locality or areas with similar characteristics (Gunter 1987). As such, those who live in deprived inner city areas with visible signs of decay are more frightened to go out alone than those living in non-urban areas (Hough 1995).

Our discussion of young people and crime also highlights the continued association between deprivation and risk of crime in late modernity. Although the evidence suggests that those groups whose members are most often apprehended for crimes (working-class males and black males) are no more likely to be involved in crime than members of other social groups, the activities of the police are organized on the premise that criminality is a subcultural phenomenon and very much related to place. One of the consequences of patterns of police surveillance is that members of disadvantaged social groups are more likely to be charged with offences and, as a result, can face difficulties in the labour market, thus increasing the odds that criminal careers will continue.

While young people are more likely to commit certain types of criminal offences than adults, many offences are relatively trivial and criminal careers usually end as young people acquire responsibilities and commitments through jobs and relationships. The main change that we have witnessed here in the last two decades concerns the implications of extended transitions. Delayed transitions are likely to result in an extension of criminality as young people have fewer responsibilities and spend greater periods of time in the company of their peers.

The other key change which is likely to have had an impact on criminality relates to the growing closeness of the relationship between youth cultures and consumerism. Whereas during the 1950s and 1960s youth was a period of affluence, especially for young people from working-class families who had relatively high disposable incomes soon after leaving school, today few young people have the same sort of access to consumer goods and some are in danger of long-term exclusion from consumer society. Although most juvenile crime is expressionistic rather than instrumental, criminologists have argued that the relative deprivation which stems from exclusion can lead to the development and prolongation of criminal careers as young people begin to appreciate that crime provides the potential for the enhancement of life-styles and the means of access to consumer culture.

Notes

1 There are significant differences in the Scottish criminal justice system and many of the policies we discuss are specific to England and Wales.
2 Cautioning is not available to the police in Scotland.

8 Politics *and* participation

Politics for most young people means a drab world of grey, be-suited,
middle-aged, middle-class, male MPs, compulsory party political
broadcasts and strange, heated arguments about which they know
little.

(MacDonald and Coffield 1991: 217)

Introduction

Although young people's lives have changed quite significantly over the last
two decades, the evidence presented in previous chapters shows that traditional forms of social stratification still hold the key to an understanding of
life chances in the age of high modernity. At the same time, we have suggested
that subjective awareness of the influence of social structures has diminished
as experiences and lifestyles become increasingly individualized. If it is true
that young people today lack a developed awareness of the significance of
collective experiences, then we would expect to find these changes reflected
in political orientations. On the surface, the task of describing changes in
the political orientations of youth appears straightforward. Yet while there
is a wealth of information on changes in the political behaviour of adults,
political scientists have tended to neglect the study of youth (Bynner and
Ashford 1994; Park 1996). Comprehensive intergenerational comparisons of
the political orientations of young people cannot be supported by the available data and consequently many of the conclusions we draw have to be
regarded as tentative.

Political commentators have frequently drawn attention to young people's lack of political awareness, to political apathy, to a disinterest in politics
and to their lack of participation in the political process (Stradling 1977;
Cochrane and Billig 1982; Furnham and Stacey 1991; Bynner and Ashford
1994). In turn, these concerns have sometimes been seen as posing a threat
to democratic traditions as young people have little basic knowledge about
political processes and remain unconvinced about the commitment of politicians to deal with issues which concern them or to act in ways which will
lead to an improvement in their circumstances (Cochrane and Billig 1982;
Bynner and Ashford 1994). Low levels of political participation among youth
have been a cause for concern in a number of industrialized countries and
in Britain and the United States of America various attempts have been made
to encourage greater involvement. The 1985 Red Wedge concert tour, for
example, aimed to encourage young people to vote for the Labour party,

while the more recent and politically neutral Rock the Vote campaign (1995) aimed to persuade young people to exercise their voting rights.

While young people's lack of involvement in the formal political process is not a new phenomenon, recent changes in the experiences of adolescents and young adults may well have an impact on forms of political engagement. In particular, given evidence showing a significant relationship between educational participation and political involvement (Bynner and Ashford 1994), changes in patterns of schooling could have an impact on political behaviour. Indeed, Emler (1996) has argued that the experiences of 16- to 25-year-olds can have a lasting and significant impact on political orientations. However, changes in the circumstances faced by young people in modern Britain can also have negative political consequences. A greater individualization of experiences in education and in the workplace can lead to a weakening of the mechanisms of political socialization, while the experience of unemployment can lead to a lack of faith in the political system, to a rise in support for extreme right and left wing parties and even to a willingness to consider violent political action (Breakwell 1986; Banks and Ullah 1987).

There is currently some debate about the extent to which young people's apparent lack of interest in politics represents a significant generational shift (Park 1996). Sociologists writing in the late-modernist tradition would argue the social changes currently taking place do not simply involve a quantitative shift in political orientations within a traditional framework, but imply a fundamental qualitative change in political values. Giddens (1991) has suggested that in high modernity an increasing emphasis is placed on life politics rather than the emancipatory politics which were associated with traditional social orders. Whereas emancipatory politics involve a struggle for liberation and the enhancement of collective life chances, life politics is the 'politics of self-actualisation in a reflexively ordered environment' (Giddens 1991: 214). In other words, the problems associated with the reflexive construction of self-identity and lifestyles involve a new set of issues and priorities which have a political nature but which link the individual to the social world in a different way. It is important to stress that Giddens is not suggesting that there is no place for emancipatory politics in late modernity. His point is that with processes of self-actualization raising fundamental moral issues, the personal sphere is increasingly linked to political issues. Items high on the agenda for life politics include issues related to nuclear power and animal rights, issues which currently concern many young people (Inglehart 1990; Bennie and Rüdig 1993; Scarbrough 1995).

In any discussion about young people and politics it is important to be aware of the different levels at which political engagement can be measured. Young people can express an interest in politics without being active in the formal institutions of party politics, they may be involved in political action while not voting or expressing a strong party affiliation, or may be knowledgeable about political issues while remaining cynical about their ability to influence the political agenda. Moreover, they may engage in actions which are political in the broader sense of the word without expressing any interest or having any involvement in the politics of emancipation. In this chapter we explore these different levels of involvement. We argue that although young people may lack an involvement in formal politics, they do have a concern with broader issues which may be construed as political and, in particular, are sometimes involved in single issue political campaigns on issues which are perceived as having a relevance to their lives. Despite these claims, we are sceptical of the tendency to regard the political priorities of youth as indicative of the ascendancy of 'post-materialist' values (Inglehart 1977, 1990) or as signalling the demise of emancipatory politics. Indeed, there is little evidence to suggest that the politics of the younger generation are very different from those of the previous generation.

Political interest and knowledge

Most recent studies of political involvement have reached the firm conclusion that young people in Britain have little interest in party politics (Banks and Ullah 1987; Roberts and Parsell 1990; Bhavnani 1991; Furnham and Stacey 1991; MacDonald and Coffield 1991; Bynner and Ashford 1994). Party politics are perceived as boring and as something which has little relevance to their lives (Banks and Ullah 1987; Roberts and Parsell 1990; Bhavnani 1991). Using evidence from the ESRC's 16–19 Initiative, Bynner and Ashford (1994) showed that more than seven in ten (72 per cent) 16-year-olds said that they were not at all interested or not very interested in politics. In contrast, recent evidence from the British Social Attitudes Survey (Park 1996) shows that around a third of adults have little or no interest in politics. Interest in politics tends to be greater among males than females (Furnham and Gunter 1983; Roberts and Parsell 1990; Furnham and Stacey 1991; Park 1996), young people from non-manual families show a greater interest than those from manual backgrounds (Roberts and Parsell 1990) and political interest tends to increase with length of education and age (Bynner and Ashford 1994; Emler 1996; Park 1996).

Faced with a lack of political interest among the younger generation, politicians have tried to sell themselves in a variety of ways and have attempted to increase their profile by appearing at events which appeal to young people. Given the high average age of British politicians (the average age of Labour MPs is currently 48 while the average age of Conservative MPs is 62; Driscoll and Kelly 1996), these efforts often look like a cynical attempt to win votes. Neil Kinnock, for example, appeared in a pop video with Tracey Ullman while at least twenty MPs including the Heritage Secretary, Virginia Bottomley, and the Leader of the Opposition, Tony Blair, attended the 1996 Brit Awards ceremony. Attempts to establish credibility with young people are not new; Harold Wilson, for example, nominated the Beatles for OBEs and appeared with them on a television show in the 1960s. Nor have these attempts been confined to British politicians. The current Rock the Vote campaign, for example, is an initiative borrowed from the US where it was successfully used to boost the turnout of young voters in the 1992 Presidential election. American political scientists accredited a 6 per cent increase in the youth vote to the campaign: votes which were largely cast in favour of Bill Clinton (Driscoll and Kelly 1996).

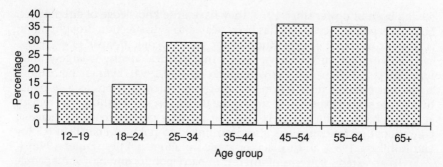

Figure 8.1 Teenagers and adults expressing a 'great deal' or 'a lot' of interest in politics
Source: Park 1996

Although young people's lack of interest in politics has been a cause for concern, Park (1996) has shown that among adults interest in politics increases with age. The 1994 British Social Attitudes Survey for the first time included a sample of teenage offspring of members of the main sample. Comparison of political interest among different age groups showed that the level of interest among the teenage sample (12- to 19-year-olds) was fairly similar to the level expressed by 18- to 24-year-olds in the main sample: those above the age of 25 appeared to be much more interested (Figure 8.1). While these figures could be used to suggest that disinterest in political issues is related to age and that the youth of today will become more interested in politics as they grow older, they could also be used to support the claim that younger people are likely to maintain a lower level of interest in politics (Park 1996). Comparing the level of interest in politics expressed by young adults who responded to the 1991 British Social Attitudes Surveys, Park (1996) argues that the level of interest expressed by 18- to 24-year-olds in 1994 was significantly lower than in 1991. In other words, although stronger evidence is needed before we are able to reach any firm conclusions, these statistics support the claim that interest in traditional politics is waning.

Young people's lack of involvement in party politics has been explained partly by a lack of knowledge as well as in terms of their apathy and cynicism (Cochrane and Billig 1982; Bhavnani 1991; MacDonald and Coffield 1991; Bynner and Ashford 1994). Many of Bhavnani's (1991) sample thought that there was no point in voting and only two of her 76 interviewees expressed an interest in politics. Similarly, Bynner and Ashford (1994) found that around a third of their sample thought that politicians were only in politics for their own ends, while more than a sixth thought that it didn't really matter which party was in power. In a study of 1,000 16-year-olds, Cochrane and Billig found that more than half of their sample regarded politics as a 'dirty business' and thought that politicians 'don't care about what ordinary people think' (1982: 291).

MacDonald and Coffield (1991) argue that young people's political apathy is partly accounted for by recent political history; with the Conservatives having been in power since 1979, they have little knowledge of alternatives. Moreover, political cynicism has been related to a disaffection brought about as a result of a lack of opportunities for young people (Marsh 1990). However, longitudinal surveys have shown that political apathy is largely unaffected by post-16 experiences (Bynner and Ashford 1994). Bynner and Ashford argue that political disaffection is something which develops as a response to negative school experiences among the under-16s; among those who remain at school beyond the age of 16, interest in party politics tends to increase. Educational performance has also been linked to political liberalism (Colby and Kohlberg 1987) and to lack of cynicism about politics (Emler 1996).

To an extent, patterns of interest in party politics among young people reflect their knowledge of the workings of the political system and it has been suggested that for a democracy to function effectively, greater emphasis needs to be placed on the provision of citizenship education within schools (Fogelman 1996). In the late 1970s the Hansard Society commissioned a survey of the political knowledge of over 4,000 15- and 16-year-olds (Stradling 1977). Boys were found to be more politically knowledgeable than girls and although there were no significant differences attributable to social class, those who attended grammar schools tended to know more about politics than those attending comprehensive schools. Yet concerns were expressed about the lack of useful political knowledge among young people with Stradling arguing that:

> There is something essentially paradoxical about a democracy in which some eighty to ninety percent of the future citizens (and present citizenry) are insufficiently well-informed about local, national and international politics to know not only what is happening but also how they are affected by it and what they can do about it. Most of the political knowledge which they do have is of a rather inert and voyeuristic kind and of little use to them either as political consumers or as political actors.
>
> (Stradling 1977: 57, quoted in Furnham and
> Gunter 1989: 19)

In the mid-1980s, Furnham and Gunter (1989) replicated a number of Stradling's questions in a survey of a smaller sample of young people. In this survey, young people were presented with a series of statements and were asked to assess which political party was likely to support a range of views. Furnham and Gunter (1989) concluded that there had been little improvement in young people's political knowledge during the previous decade. Their results also indicated that boys and middle-class respondents were more likely to produce the correct answers. Furnham and Gunter (1989) showed that while the vast majority of young people were able to name the Prime Minister (95 per cent) and the Leader of the Opposition (86 per cent), less than half could name the Home Secretary (49 per cent) and just one in five (20 per cent) could correctly state the number of MPs (635); 22 per cent of respondents thought that there were 140 MPs in the House of Commons.

More recently, a short quiz about politics was used in the teenage sample

(12- to 19-year-olds) linked to the British Social Attitudes Survey. While most of the respondents correctly answered the majority of questions, analysis of the results showed that males knew more about party politics than females, and those from non-manual social classes performed better than those from manual families. There was no significant difference in the political knowledge of Labour and Conservative supporters, but supporters of the Liberal Democrats displayed the greatest knowledge of the political system (Park 1996).

Political participation

Although young people may have a poor knowledge of political institutions and remain cynical about political processes, Bhavnani has suggested that cynicism does not necessarily imply apathy or a lack of interest in broader political issues. Indeed, she argues that cynicism 'may even act as an impetus for political activity' (1991: 13) by citing a study by Jackson (1973) showing that among black law students in the US, the most cynical were the most politically active. Nevertheless, in terms of participation in the formal political process, young people's professed lack of interest in politics is reflected in levels of party membership and their voting behaviour. Statistics on the membership of the main political parties in Britain show that young people's impression that party politics is largely the preserve of the middle-aged is correct. More than two-thirds of the members of the Conservative party (67 per cent), over a half of Liberal Democrats (52 per cent) and more than a third (35 per cent) of Labour party members are over the age of 55. Although the Green party has a lower age profile, nearly one in five members are over 55 (18 per cent) (Figure 8.2) (Bennie *et al.* 1996). Among all of the main political parties, a very small proportion of members are under 25; ranging from 1 per cent of Conservative members to 12 per cent of the Greens.

Young people are also less likely than adults to register a vote and tend to have a weaker commitment to any political party (Heath *et al.* 1991). In 1992, the names of more than a million 18- to 24-year-olds were absent from the electoral register and the British Election Survey shows that levels of voting were lowest among this age group. While levels of voting were similar among males and females (75 per cent and 76 per cent respectively), rates of participation were higher among non-manual employees (80 per cent) compared to manual workers (72 per cent) and lowest among those who had never had a job (69 per cent).

Reliable figures on the electoral behaviour of young people are difficult to obtain and even the most influential political commentators fail to agree on the direction of the youth vote in the last general election. Butler and Kavanagh (1992), for example, argue that in the 1992 general election, 39 per cent of 18- to 24-year-olds voted Labour, 35 per cent voted Conservative and 19 per cent cast their vote in favour of the Liberal Democrats. In contrast, Sanders (1992) argues that among the same age group, 38 per cent voted Conservative, 35 per cent Labour and 22 per cent Liberal Democrat. Figures from the 1992 British Election Survey provide another source of variation, suggesting that equal proportions of young people voted for the Labour and

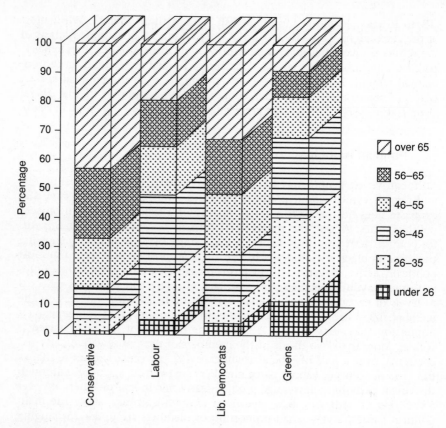

Figure 8.2 The age of party members
Source: Bennie *et al.* 1996

Conservative parties (36 per cent).[1] Despite these differences, British political scientists tend to agree that younger voters are less likely than older ones to vote Conservative and more likely to vote for the Labour party, a tendency which has long been apparent (Butler and Kavanagh 1992; Sanders 1992). However, according to Sanders, young voters in 1992 were more pro-Conservative than their counterparts in 1987, a difference which he regards as a consequence of their 'political socialization during an unbroken period of Conservative government' (1992: 190).

Political scientists frequently regard age-related differences in voting behaviour as being part of a 'life cycle' effect whereby older people are seen as becoming more conservative (Sanders 1992). In this respect, the political behaviour of today's youth is entirely predictable. Indeed, a recent comparison of party support among parents and their children showed that although teenagers were more likely than their parents to support the Labour party and less likely to support the Conservatives, differences were quite small (Park 1996). Indeed, Park (1996) shows that almost two-thirds (65 per cent) of young people with a parent who identified with the Conservatives held the same political allegiances, while nearly three-quarters (74 per cent) of teenage Labour supporters had a parent who supported Labour. Although a significant proportion of young people hold different allegiances to those of their parents, Himmelweit and colleagues (1985) have argued that in cases where parents hold political views which are in line with their class member-ship, young people tend to follow their parents' political views. Evidence from the 1992 British Election Survey also shows that traditional socioeconomic dif-ferences in voting patterns were clearly visible among 18- to 24-year-olds; those in manual occupations or unemployed tended to favour the Labour party while those in non-manual occupations or in full-time education favoured the Conservatives.

With evidence that the main predictors of partisanship among adults (such as social class, level of education, gender and 'race') also help us to understand the party affiliation of young voters, it is tempting to argue that sources of continuity in the political system are more powerful than sources of change. However, there have been important changes in patterns of polit-ical socialization which could serve to weaken these links. Franklin (1985) studied the effect of parents' social class and parents' party affiliation on vot-ing behaviour and argued that, in Britain, such effects became weaker between the 1960s and late 1970s. Heath and colleagues (1991) undertook a similar analysis for voting patterns between 1964 and 1987 and argued that children had become less likely to adopt the political perspectives of their parents. As yet there is no evidence to show whether this trend is continuing, although changing levels of educational participation may have an ongoing impact on processes of political socialization (Scarbrough 1995; Emler 1996).

While the increase in educational participation may have an impact on party allegiances, changes in processes of political socialization have also been affected by the restructuring of the youth labour market. Traditionally, working-class youth received a swift initiation into the world of politics on the factory floor through conversations with older workmates and through union membership. However, as MacDonald and Coffield point out

the cultural inheritance of collectivism, trade union membership and Labour Party support, traditionally bound to apprenticeships into manual labour, are swiftly being eroded by the new cultural identities con-structed over the past decade through youth traineeships.

(1991: 220)

Greater insecurity in the labour market and the uncertainties which char-acterize youth training can mean that young people's work experiences are more individualized as they are forced to compete with each other in the hope of remaining in employment. Thus the apparent increase in Conservat-ive support among young voters is likely to be one of the consequences of young workers being less able to identify collectivist solutions to negative workplace experiences.

Although evidence of a link between educational participation and po-litical involvement has been interpreted as a factor leading to a greater and more informed participation in the political process (Heath and Topf 1987; Bynner and Ashford 1994), others would argue that benefits are partly dependent on opportunities in the youth labour market. Indeed, if the efforts young people make in the education system are not rewarded through entry into highly paid or high status jobs, the likely outcome of this status inconsistency will be a rise in dissatisfaction leading to political unrest and protest among those who consider that they have been denied access to appropriate opportunities (Runciman 1966; Emler 1996). However, this interpretation has been challenged by Abrams (1990) who argues that Runciman's theory of a causal link between the relative deprivation of individuals and social protest is flawed. Abrams suggests that on an individual level, thwarted ambition (even if perceived as unfair or unjustified) leads to stress rather than political unrest. Drawing on the work of Tajfel and Turner (1979), Abrams (1990) suggests that it is *group*, rather than *individual*, relative deprivation that leads to social change. In other words, for political action to occur, people have to develop an awareness that a group to which they belong is being illegitimately disadvantaged. Abrams illustrates this by reference to the rise of Scottish nationalism which he regards as underpinned by a collective feeling that the Scots have been subject to discrimination by the English. Linking this theory to potential for political action among youth, Abrams suggests that current trends in education and the labour market may actually have weakened the potential for collectivism by strengthening individualist sentiments.

In communities characterized by high unemployment and urban decline, some young people may develop an awareness that the group to which they belong has been unfairly disadvantaged. Indeed, those faced with insecurity in the labour market, who are deprived of traditional sources of political socialization and who maintain a cynical attitude to mainstream political parties may come to identify with parties on the extreme right or left. In particular, the popularity of the National Front among working-class males has been associated with the increase in unemployment, with members tending to be drawn from the least educated sections of the population. Roberts and Parsell (1990), for example, argued that support for extreme politics of the left or right was strongest in high unemployment areas; in Liverpool, more young people supported extreme left or right wing parties than the Conservatives (9 per cent supported Militant while 8 per cent supported the National Front). Cochrane and Billig (1983) showed that in the West Midlands a rise in unemployment corresponded with a sharp increase in support for the National Front among young working-class males (from 4 per cent in 1980 to 15 per cent in 1983). Indeed, they argued that racism was widespread throughout their (largely working-class) cohort and manifest in support for the National Front and the British Movement. Moreover, supporters of extreme right wing parties were more politically alienated than supporters of the mainstream parties and tended to feel that politicians took no notice of the concerns of ordinary people. Perhaps as a consequence, more than four in ten (45 per cent) young National Front and British Movement supporters felt that violence was a justified means of bringing about changes, compared to three in ten (30 per cent) Labour and Conservative supporters (Cochrane and Billig 1982).

Despite claims that rising unemployment is likely to lead to political extremism, a number of writers have been critical of the idea that negative labour market experiences are leading to a new radicalism (Banks and Ullah 1987; Roberts and Parsell 1990). Roberts and Parsell (1990) argue that unemployment is more likely to lead to 'passive alienation', which can be manifest in vandalism and conflicts with the police (see Chapter 7) rather than political unrest. They suggest that experiences in the post-school period have little impact on political orientations. Indeed, responses to unemployment are more likely to be individualist (such as stress and self-blame) rather than collectivist; the unemployed young people studied by Banks and Ullah (1987), for example, failed to identify a collective solution to their problems. With increasing levels of unemployment in the 1980s, the Conservatives were hated by the vast majority of the long-term unemployed (McRae 1987), although the majority of young unemployed voted for the Labour party rather than for extreme parties of the left or right.

Post-materialist politics

Another theme which has been pursued by political scientists relates quite closely to Giddens's distinction between emancipatory politics and life politics. Inglehart (1977, 1990) has claimed to be able to detect a shift from 'materialist' to 'post-materialist' value orientations within advanced industrial societies and suggests that these changes have had an impact on the political agenda and on forms of political affiliation which can be seen as 'displacing the politics of class' (Scarbrough 1995: 123). These ideas are based on the theory that individuals become more concerned with self-actualization (post-modernist values) once concerns about basic needs and securities (materialism) have been fulfilled. Thus materialist values are centred around the need for physical sustenance and safety, whereas post-materialist values stress the need for belonging, self-expression and quality of life. In sum, these writers claim to be able to identify a 'silent revolution' which 'originates in the different value priorities as between older and younger generations, which, as younger generations replace older generations, result in a slow but steady shift in the cultural character of a society' (Scarbrough 1995: 125).

Both Inglehart (1990) and Scarbrough (1995) have attempted to examine the extent to which a shift from materialist to post-materialist values can be detected empirically through an examination of the value orientations of members of different birth cohorts. Both writers detected a growth in post-materialist values which they linked, in part, to rising levels of education. In this respect, differences between the values of younger and older generations are not simply understood as representing 'youthful idealism' (Abramson and Inglehart 1992: 200), but reflect the material circumstances of the 'unprecedented' historical period (Scarbrough 1995: 148) in which the current generation of young people spent their formative years. Although the ideas of Inglehart are controversial, they are central to our discussion of young people and politics in late modernity in so far as Giddens has suggested that political priorities have changed in the light of global insecurities.[2]

If we were to accept Giddens's interpretation of trends in high modernity, we would stress young people's relative lack of involvement in emancipatory politics, as represented by the mainstream political parties, and would highlight their interest and involvement in lifestyle politics. While young people may express an interest in single issue campaigns, such as environmental issues, animal rights and the peace movement (Bennie and Rüdig 1993), we do not regard this as a generational shift. In the 1950s and 1960s, for example, young people were active in CND and in protests against American involvement in Vietnam. Indeed, the important changes which have occurred can be interpreted as being essentially conservative; whereas single issue movements which attracted young people once subscribed to a broader vision of social and economic change (usually a variant of socialism), today that broader social critique is often absent.

It is true that environmental movements frequently have a vision of a new society in which capitalistic expansion would be limited and which revolve around a post-materialist philosophy. Indeed, the interest of young people in environmental politics has been interpreted by some as part of this intergenerational shift from materialist to post-materialist values identified by Inglehart (1977, 1990). Inglehart (1977) suggests that whereas the older generation regard reindustrialization and rearmament as important, shifts in values would lead to the emergence of a new type of political protest based on issues surrounding the quality of life and to a reduction in class conflict. The Green party has had some success in involving young people (Rüdig *et al.* 1991; Banks 1993; Bennie and Rüdig 1993). However, although there was a large increase in young members of the Green party around 1989, many subsequently left what they came to perceive (correctly) as an adult dominated organization (Banks 1993).[3] Indeed, with low levels of political activity among young members, Bennie and Rüdig (1993) suggest that membership frequently represented a fashion statement rather than reflecting serious involvement. In this respect it can be argued that young people's involvement in post-materialist politics is somewhat limited. Bennie and Rüdig (1993) also examined the views of young people and adults on a wide range of issues related to the local, national and global environments; concern was widespread, but the differences between adults and young people tended to be small. However, on a practical level, there were interesting differences in emphasis; young people were more likely to purchase 'green' products, while adults were more concerned with conserving resources.

The involvement of young people in new social movements can also be used to test the proposition that life politics are becoming more important than emancipatory politics. Over the last two decades, a number of seemingly diverse movements have developed which have been seen as sharing similar underlying values. The term new social movements has been used by a number of sociologists (e.g. Cohen 1983; Touraine 1985; Lash and Urry 1987; Scott 1990) to draw attention to the ways in which a range of groups (such as CND, Friends of the Earth, Animal Liberation Front, Gay Rights and New Age Travellers) have emerged which pose a challenge to the established political, social and economic order of advanced capitalist societies. Those who are a part of the new social movements are frequently young, often have parents employed in the public or service sectors of the economy and many participants occupy peripheral positions in the labour market (such as students and the unemployed) (Hallsworth 1994).[4]

Hallsworth (1994) has argued that two distinct categories of new social movements can be identified: those which seek to defend the natural and social environment against perceived threats (such as environmental and anti-nuclear movements) and which have sought to politicize such issues, and those which seek the extension of social rights to groups which have been repressed by state action (such as gay rights and feminist movements). For Lash and Urry (1987), new social movements reflect the emergence of a set of values and political standpoints which are critical of the state and of its ability to promote meaningful social change. Thus the politics of the new generation are seen as highlighting the disintegration of older forms of collective identity, a politicization of the 'personal' and a rejection of forms of politics rooted in the old social order rather than a disinterest in politics *per se*.

On the other hand, it is important to keep these changes in perspective. In the recent British Social Attitudes Survey, just 6 per cent of 12- to 19-year-olds supported the Green party while in the last general election a large majority of under 25-year-olds who voted cast their votes in favour of one of the mainstream political parties. In other words, while young people may get involved in political causes, especially where proposed action is seen as affecting their personal security (e.g. nuclear weapons) or freedom (e.g. the Criminal Justice Bill) we do not predict a significant weakening of collective, emancipatory politics. Indeed, the politics of self-actualization are unlikely to thrive in an economic context characterized by uncertainty and high unemployment.

Conclusion

If young people are to be regarded as a vanguard of social change (Feuer 1969), then the evidence we have reviewed in this chapter suggests that the future is essentially conservative. The family remains central to processes of political socialization and to a large extent young people come to share the political concerns of their parents (Allatt and Benson 1991; Park 1996). Although there is some evidence that the younger generation has a weaker commitment to traditional party politics, existing data does not support the conclusion that political orientations among the young have become individualized. Young people do express collective concerns, but frequently seek personal solutions to problems which are largely a consequence of their socioeconomic positions. In this context Abrams (1990) is correct to suggest that disadvantage which is interpreted individually leads to stress rather than political unrest. On the other hand, the disadvantages faced by some groups of young people are so strong that they cannot fail to link them to the broader economic structure; in these circumstances, parties of the extreme right or left may be seen as offering the only real solution.

Although we reject the claim that in late modernity life politics come to assume a central position, we suggest that some of the political priorities which have emerged in recent years reflect the new risks and global insecurities which Giddens (1991) has highlighted. However, these are concerns which call for emancipation from perceived threats to the quality of life in high modernity rather than being linked to processes of self-actualization. Nevertheless, life politics and empancipatory politics are closely intertwined and, as Beck (1992) suggests, political movements can simultaneously engage in struggles to reduce global risks as well as promoting the right to develop alternative lifestyles.

Notes

1 The problems of comparability seem to arise from sampling errors. Many post-election surveys are based on samples which are too small to make accurate statements about the voting patterns of small age-based subsets. Being based on a sample of 3,534, the British Election Survey is perhaps least likely to be affected by sampling error.
2 One of the major criticisms of Inglehart relates to the tendency for the shift from materialist to post-materialist values to continue irrespective of fluctuations in economic prosperity.
3 Rüdig and colleagues (1991) show that the average age of new Green party members was 38.
4 Many new social movements appeal to a broad age range. Friends of the Earth and CND, for example, have many middle-aged members.

9 *The* epistemological fallacy *of* late modernity

> Class location is a basic determinant of the matrix of objective possibilities faced by individuals, the real alternatives people face in making decisions.
>
> (Wright 1985: 144)

Introduction

The experiences of young people growing up in the late 1990s are quite different from those encountered by earlier generations, but we are not convinced that recent social changes have been conceptualized in a way which fully enlightens us about the nature of these developments. Life in late modernity involves subjective discomfort and uncertainty. Young people can struggle to establish adult identities and maintain coherent biographies, they may develop strategies to overcome various obstacles, but their life chances remain highly structured with social class and gender being crucial to an understanding of experiences in a range of life contexts.

In our view, late modernity involves an essential continuity with the past; economic and cultural resources are still central to an understanding of differential life chances and experiences. In this context we have suggested that life in late modernity revolves around an epistemological fallacy. The paradox of late modernity is that although the collective foundations of social life have become more obscure, they continue to provide powerful frameworks which constrain young people's experiences and life chances. Over the last two decades a number of changes have occurred which have helped to obscure these continuities, promoting individual responsibilities and weakening collectivist traditions. In this chapter, we highlight the main sources of change and continuity in the lives of young people, discuss some of the ways in which their subjective understanding of the world can be seen to misrepresent these underlying structures and suggest that the work of Elias (1978, 1982) provides the key to a more adequate conceptualization of the changes which we have described.

The crossroads of social reproduction

If there is empirical evidence to support the claim that we are currently witnessing an historical transformation of the social world, then we would expect to find the most advanced representation of these changes in the experiences of young people at the crossroads of the process of social reproduction. In our view young people's life contexts have changed significantly over the last two decades, changes that are closely linked to the transformation of the youth labour market which was part of a broader process of economic change in Western economies, involving a shift from manufacturing to service industries. The recession of the late 1970s and early 1980s was a turning point, signifying a shift from a Fordist to a post-Fordist industrial structure which was marked by a radical change in the demand for youth labour. During the Fordist era, there was a demand for relatively unqualified school-leavers in large industrial units; since the mid-1980s patterns of labour demand have changed significantly and opportunities for young workers are increasingly located in small work units. The demand for 'flexible specialization' and the increased use of part-time and temporary employment contracts have weakened collective employment experiences and can be associated with a process of individualization and a sense of insecurity and risk.

The restructuring of the youth labour market during the 1980s also led to demands for more advanced educational qualifications and different types of skills which, in turn, meant that the average age at which young people entered the labour market increased. These changes led to a greater protraction and diversification of transitions from school to work so that by the late 1980s, young people tended to follow a wider and very different set of routes into the labour market. Unemployment and training schemes became part of the transitional experiences of a growing proportion of young people. Although transitional routes remained highly stratified, these changes again affected subjective orientations as the range of experiences encountered at this stage in the life cycle became much more unique.

Although changing school to work transitions have led to an increased risk of marginalization, risks continue to be distributed in a way which reflect social divisions characteristic of the traditional order. In other words, it is still possible to predict labour market outcomes fairly accurately on the basis of social class (via educational performance) and gender. Indeed, while the breakdown of collective transitions created the illusion of individuality, we have argued that these changes have had little effect on processes of social reproduction.

In both Fordist and post-Fordist economies, patterns of social reproduction are mediated through educational attainment and, partly as a result of changes in the youth labour market, educational experiences have been transformed over the last two decades. Young people remain in full-time education for significantly longer periods and follow a more diverse set of educational routes in which consumer choice is seen as playing an increasingly significant part. This increased emphasis on credentials, choice, and the greater social mix within educational institutions can be seen as having weakened collective responses to the school and can also be associated with a process of individualization. Yet despite the far reaching nature of changing educational experiences, the relationship between social class and scholastic performance has not weakened significantly. However, there has been a marked improvement in the educational prospects of females, changes which are likely to have been influenced by changing expectations of parent and teachers and which reflect the growth of opportunities in the female labour market.

With the rapid expansion in post-compulsory educational participation and the protraction of school to work transitions, young people today spend longer periods of time in a state of semi-dependency. In recent years, legislative changes have been introduced which have served to reinforce the extension of semi-dependency, making it more difficult for young people to make early housing or domestic transitions. These changing patterns of dependency have also helped promote a greater diversity of experiences. Males and females from all social classes tend to marry later and are increasingly likely to spend time living in intermediate households. Despite these changes, the timing of domestic and housing transitions and the chances of successful completion still reflect traditional class and gender divisions. Whereas the protraction of domestic and housing transitions has created the potential for young people to develop as individuals and experiment with different living arrangements, new forms of vulnerability have also been introduced due to the removal of state support and the increasing unreliability of access to family resources. In this context we have suggested that the establishment of adult identities has become more problematic.

While experiences of the three main youth transitions continue to reflect class and gender divisions, in other areas of young people's lives differences are not so clear cut and there is evidence of a degree of convergence. In particular, a number of writers have drawn attention to the lack of significant differences in leisure and lifestyles. The relationship between class and youth cultures has all but vanished and gender differences have weakened. This convergence partly reflects the extension of youth as a stage in the life cycle with young people from all social classes being denied access to enhanced resources through employment. However, changing leisure patterns and lifestyles also highlight the extent to which preferences have been manufactured through mass marketing techniques. In other words, lifestyles are increasingly shaped by the market and therefore should not be viewed as an expression of individual choice. Moreover, those who lack the resources to participate in consumer markets face cultural as well as financial exclusion; in this respect, our evidence highlights a polarization of social life in which those occupying disadvantaged socioeconomic positions face the prospect of total exclusion.

The evidence we reviewed on changes in the health and health related behaviour of young people also highlighted a relative absence of significant class-related differences, although we suggested that youth could be viewed as a period of dormancy. We were not convinced that the relative lack of class-related differences in youth would be manifest in health equality in adulthood. Nevertheless, there is evidence that the uncertainties which stem from changing transitional experiences are having a negative impact on young people's mental health. Suicidal thoughts and parasuicide have increased, while, especially for young women, eating disorders can be seen as an attempt to control identity and body image in a period when scope for meaningful action is limited.

The protraction of youth transitions can also be linked to a prolongation of involvement in criminal activity. Although survey evidence highlights a lack of class and gender differentials in patterns of participation in illegal activities, apprehensions and convictions remain heavily concentrated among working-class males and members of ethnic minorities. In turn, the extension of criminal careers, which can result from exclusion from labour markets and fashions relating to lifestyle consumption, can lead to the increased vulnerability of those occupying disadvantaged positions within traditional social structures.

Changes in education and the labour market can also be linked to changes in political orientations. In particular, the weakening of collective traditions is likely to have an impact on processes of political socialization and it has been argued that these changes have already been manifest in a swing towards the Conservatives among young voters. However, as the evidence on trends in young people's political behaviour is somewhat weak, we believe that such conclusions may be premature. While young people tend to display a lack of interest in politics and while their knowledge of formal political processes is underdeveloped, political knowledge, interest and affiliation still reflects their location within traditional social structures. A number of writers, including Anthony Giddens, have suggested that the growth of new social movements represents a shift away from emancipatory politics based on class divisions and the emergence of life politics in which priority is given to processes of self-actualization. However, although young people are often associated with single issue political campaigns, we are sceptical of the way in which the political priorities of young people have been seen as indicative of a greater emphasis on post-materialist values. Indeed, in our view young people's political involvement and orientations highlight an essential conservatism and reveal important continuities with the past.

Conceptualizing late modernity

The existence of powerful continuities which link the experiences of this generation to those of earlier ones mean that we are cautious about attaching too much significance to changes which have occurred during the last two decades. Throughout this book we have argued that the social divisions which were seen as shaping life chances in modernity are still central to an understanding of structured inequalities in late modernity. Young people's experiences are strongly affected by gender divisions, and even though we have focused on the lives of young people in a period of rapid social change, there is little evidence to suggest that the effect of social class on life chances is diminishing. At the same time, we are willing to accept that social divisions have become more obscure due to a greater individualization of experiences. This increasing lack of awareness of the significance of social interdependencies leads us to share the conclusions of Goldthorpe and Marshall (1992) who have argued that social classes should not be seen as the basis for collective action and consciousness or regarded as an engine of social change. However, for us, capitalism without classes is inconceivable because some groups are always able to monopolize scarce resources and ensure that these advantages are reproduced across generations.

While we have rejected suggestions that traditional social divisions are becoming less powerful determinants of life chances, we do accept Beck's conclusion that one of the central characteristics of late modernity is a weakening of collective social identities. Indeed, in our view the process of individualization represents a subjective weakening of social bonds due to a growing diversity of life experiences. These changes are reflected in an individualization of lifestyles and a convergence of class cultures. However, we are critical of the significance which both Beck and Giddens attach to changes in the ways individuals interpret the world and subjectively construct social realities. In our view, Giddens and, to a lesser extent, Beck, have failed to capture the essence of late modernity due to an overemphasis on the significance of individual reflexivity. While we can identify many common concerns and points of agreement between Beck and Giddens, we share the concern that in Giddens's recent work 'subjects appear . . . to be disconnected from their "real" social and political contexts' as a result of an overestimation of the extent to which individuals are able to construct their identities (May and Cooper 1995: 75).

Giddens's susceptibility to the epistemological fallacy of late modernity is particularly evident in his argument about the declining significance of area. Giddens suggests that the worlds young people inhabit are no longer bounded by space and argues that their experiences are broadened by continual access to mass communications systems. Consequently, place loses much of its significance as experiences are shaped by much broader social processes in time and space. As Giddens puts it, 'place becomes phantasmagoric . . . [it] . . . becomes thoroughly penetrated by disembedding mechanisms which recombine the local activities into time–space relations of ever-widening scope' (1991: 146). While we accept that mediated experiences are central to an understanding of late modernity, in our view its main significance is derived from its power to *distort* reality. The television, for example, can open a window on a world which is remote from our lived experiences, programmes can help shape our opinions and may make us feel a part of the broader community. At the same time, our opportunities and our life chances continue to be structured by our lived rather than our mediated experiences.

In contrast to the work of Giddens, Beck constantly draws attention to the ways in which processes of individualization are tightly constrained. Thus in his most recent book it is argued that

> coupled with this interest in 'the individual solution' there is however considerable pressure to conform and behave in a standardized way; the means which encourage individualism also induce sameness . . . The situations which arise are contradictory because double-faced: individual decisions are heavily dependent on outside influences.
>
> (Beck and Beck-Gernsheim 1995: 40)

Thus the process of individualization can be linked to long-term developmental trends. In education and in the labour market, young people are forced to take greater individual responsibility and to assess appropriate courses of action. Risk and uncertainty are the consequences of pressures to adopt individualistic perspectives in a society characterized by interdependency.

The contradiction which Beck highlights here has been examined in detail by Norbert Elias (1978, 1982). In rejecting the dualism between the self and the outside world, Elias argued that individuals are tied together by chains of mutual dependence to form changeable social figurations. Thus individuals are inseparable from their social contexts and as social figurations change, similar changes are manifest in the constituent parts. According to Elias, the idea that the individual represented a separable, independent, social entity is a product of long-term historical trends which have involved an increase in self-control and a reduction in externally imposed discipline. In this sense, individualization can be regarded as an historical extension of a process which led first to the emergence of what Elias refers to as *homo clausus*, or closed-off individualism. Building on these ideas, late modernity can be seen as representing a further step along a continuum leading from collectivized to individualized social identities. Seen in these terms, social change does not involve a weakening of social structures, the chains of interdependence remain intact, but 'the entire complex of intermeshing processes of change eludes the control and even the comprehension of the individuals who partake in it' (Goudsblom 1977: 148).

In other words, life in high modernity revolves around an epistemological fallacy in which feeling of separation from the collectivity represents part of a long-term historical process which is closely associated with subjective perceptions of risk and uncertainty. Individuals are forced to negotiate a set of risks which impinge on all aspects of their daily lives, yet the intensification of individualism means that crises are perceived as individual shortcomings rather than the outcome of processes which are largely outside the control of individuals. In this context, we have seen that some of the problems faced by young people in modern Britain stem from an attempt to negotiate difficulties on an individual level. Blind to the existence of powerful chains of interdependency, young people frequently attempt to resolve collective problems through individual action and hold themselves responsible for their inevitable failure.

References

Abma, R. (1992) 'Working class heroes. A review of the youth subculture theory of the Centre for Contemporary Cultural Studies', in W. Meeus, M. de Goede, W. Kox and K. Hurrelman (eds) *Adolescent Careers and Cultures*. Berlin: de Gruyter.

Abrams, D. (1990) *Political Identity. Relative Deprivation, Social Identity and the Case of Scottish Nationalism*, ESRC 16–19 Initiative Occasional Papers, No. 24. London: City University.

Abrams, M. (1961) *The Teenage Consumer*. London: London Press Exchange.

Abramson, P.A. and Inglehart, R. (1992) 'Generational replacement and value change in eight west European societies', *British Journal of Political Science*, 22: 183–228.

Adams, J. (1995) *Risk*. London: University College London.

Adler, M., Petch, A. and Tweedie, J. (1989) *Parental Choice and Educational Policy*. Edinburgh: Edinburgh University Press.

Ainley, P. (1991) *Young People Leaving Home*. London: Cassell.

Alcohol Concern (1991) *Warning. Alcohol Can Damage Your Health*. London: Alcohol Concern.

Allatt, P. and Benson, L. (1991) *Family Discourse. Political Socialization Amongst Teenagers and their Families*. ESRC 16–19 Initiative Occasional Papers, No. 37. London: City University.

Allen-Mills, T. (1996) 'Straw's crime-busting curfew is just an American dream', *Sunday Times*, 9 June.

Anderson, I., Kemp, P. and Quilgars, D. (1993) *Single Homeless People*. London: HMSO.

Anderson, S., Kinsey, R., Loader, I. and Smith, C. (1994) *Cautionary Tales. Young People, Crime and Policing in Edinburgh*. Aldershot: Avebury.

Aries, P. (1962) *Centuries of Childhood. A Social History of Family Life*. London: Cape.

Ashton, D.N. (1986) *Unemployment Under Capitalism*. Brighton: Wheatsheaf.

Ashton, D.N. and Field, D. (1976) *Young Workers*. London: Hutchinson.

Ashton, D.N., Maguire, M.J. and Garland, V. (1982) *Youth in the Labour Market*. London: Department of Employment.

Ashton, D. N., Maguire, M.J. and Spilsbury, M. (1990) *Restructuring the Labour Market. The Implications for Youth*. Basingstoke: Macmillan.

Atkinson, J. (1984) 'Manpower strategies for flexible organizations', *Personnel Management*, August: 28–32.

Auld, J., Dorn, N. and South, N. (1986) 'Irregular work, irregular pleasures. Heroin in the 1980s', in R. Matthews and J. Young (eds) *Confronting Crime*. London: Sage.

Babb, P. and Bethare, A. (1995) 'Trends in births and marriage', *Population Trends*, 81: 17–22.

Bagguley, P. and Mann, K. (1992) 'Idle thieving bastards? Scholarly representations of the underclass', *Work, Employment and Society*, 6: 113–26.

Bagnall, G. and Plant, M.A. (1991) 'AIDS risks, alcohol and illicit drug use amongst young adults in areas of high and low rates of HIV infection', *AIDS Care*, 3: 355–61.

Balding, J. (1993) *Young People in 1992*. Schools Health Education Unit, Exeter: Exeter University School of Education.

Ball, S.J. (1981) *Beachside Comprehensive. A Case Study of Secondary Schooling*. Cambridge: Cambridge University Press.

Ball, S.J., Bowe, R. and Gerwitz, S. (1996) 'School choice, social class and distinction. The realization of social advantage in education', *Journal of Educational Policy*, 11: 89–113.

Banks, M.H. and Jackson, P.R. (1982) 'Unemployment and risk of minor psychiatric disorders in young people. Cross sectional and longitudinal evidence', *Psychological Medicine*, 12: 789–98.

Banks, M.H. and Ullah, P. (1987) 'Political attitudes and voting among unemployed and employed youth', *Journal of Adolescence*, 10: 201–16.

Banks, M.H. and Ullah, P. (1988) *Youth Unemployment in the 1980s. Its Psychological Effects*. Beckenham: Croom Helm.

Banks, M.H., Bates, I., Breakwell, G., Bynner, J., Emler, N., Jamieson, L. and Roberts, K. (1992) *Careers and Identities*. Buckingham: Open University Press.

Banks, S. (1993) 'Young people and the environment', *Youth and Policy*, 42: 1–5.

Baudrillard, J. (1988) *Selected Writings*. Oxford: Oxford University Press.

Bauman, Z. (1988) *Freedom*. Milton Keynes: Open University Press.

Beck, U. (1992) *Risk Society. Towards a New Modernity*. London: Sage.

Beck, U. (1994) 'The reinvention of politics. Towards a theory of reflexive modernization', in U. Beck, A. Giddens and S. Lash (eds) *Reflexive Modernization. Politics, Tradition and Aesthetics in the Modern Social Order*. Oxford: Polity.

Beck, U. and Beck-Gernsheim, E. (1995) *The Normal Chaos of Love*. Oxford: Polity.

Bell, C., Howieson, C., King, K. and Raffe, D. (1988) *Liaisons Dangereuses? Education–Industry Relationship in the First Scottish TVEI Projects*. Sheffield: The Training Agency.

Bell, D. (1973) *The Coming of Post-Industrial Society*. New York: Basic Books.

Bennett, D. and Williams, M. (1994) 'Adolescent health care. The international context', in R. S. Tonkin (ed.) *Current Issues in the Adolescent Patient*. London: Baillière Tindall.

Bennie, L., Curtice, J. and Rüdig, W. (1996) 'Party members', in D. McIver (ed.) *Liberal Democrats*. Hemel Hempstead: Harvester Weatsheaf.

Bennie, L. and Rüdig, W. (1993) 'Youth and the environment. Attitudes and actions in the 1990s', *Youth and Policy*, 42: 1–5.

Berger, P.L., Berger, B. and Kellner, H. (1974) *The Homeless Mind*. Harmondsworth: Penguin.

Bhavnani, K.-K. (1991) *Talking Politics. A Psychological Framing for Views from Youth in Britain*. Cambridge: Cambridge University Press.

Biggart, A. and Furlong, A. (1996) 'Educating "discouraged workers". Cultural diversity in the upper secondary school', *British Journal of Sociology of Education*, 17: 253–66.

Blackburn, R.M. and Jarman, J. (1993) 'Changing inequalities in access to British universities', *Oxford Review of Education*, 9: 197–215.

Blackman, S.J. (1987) 'The labour market in school. New vocationalism and issues of socially ascribed discrimination', in P. Brown and D.N. Ashton (eds) *Education, Unemployment and Labour Markets*. London: Falmer.

Boskind-Lodahl, M. (1976) 'Cinderella's stepsisters. A feminist perspective on anorexia and bulimia', *Signs: Journal of Women, Culture and Society*, 2: 342–56.

Boudon, R. (1973) *Education, Opportunity and Social Inequality*. New York: Wiley.

Bourdieu, P. (1977) 'Cultural reproduction and social reproduction', in J. Karabel and A.H. Halsey (eds) *Power and Ideology in Education*. New York: Oxford University Press.

Bourdieu, P. (1986) *Distinction. A Social Critique of the Judgement of Taste*. London: Routledge.

Bourdieu, P. and Passeron, J.C. (1977) *Reproduction in Education, Society and Culture*. London: Sage.

Box, S., Hale, C. and Andrews, G. (1988) Explaining the fear of crime, *British Journal of Criminology*, 28: 340–56.

Breakwell, G. (1986) 'Political and attributional responses of the young short-term unemployed', *Political Psychology*, 7: 265–78.

Breakwell, G. (1992) 'Changing patterns of sexual behaviour in 16–29-year-olds in the UK. A cohort-sequential longitudinal study', in W. Meeus, M. de Goede, W. Kox and K. Hurrelmann (eds) *Adolescent Careers and Cultures*. Berlin: de Gruyter.

Brewers Society (1990) *Statistical Handbook*. London: Brewers Society.

Brown, P. (1987) *Schooling Ordinary Kids*. London: Tavistock.

Brown, P. (1990) 'Schooling and economic life in the UK', in L. Chisholm, P. Büchner, H.-H. Krüger and P. Brown (eds) *Childhood, Youth and Social Change: A Comparative Perspective*. London: Falmer.

Brown, P. (1995) 'Cultural capital and social exclusion: some observations on recent trends in education, employment and the labour market', *Work, Employment and Society*, 9(1): 29–51.

Brown, P. and Lauder, H. (1996) Education, globalisation and economic development, *Journal of Education Policy*, 11: 1–27.

Brown, P. and Scase, R. (1994) *Higher Education and Corporate Realities. Class Culture and the Decline of Graduate Careers*. London: University College London.

Brownfield, D. (1996) 'Subcultural theories of crime and delinquency', in J. Hagan, A.R. Gillis and D. Brownfield (eds) *Criminological Controversies*. Oxford: Westview.

Büchner, P. (1990) 'Growing up in the eighties. Changes in the social biography of childhood in the FRG', in L. Chisholm, P. Büchner, H.-H. Krüger and P. Brown (eds) *Childhood, Youth and Social Change. A Comparative Perspective*. London: Falmer.

Burghes, L. (1994) *Lone Parenthood and Family Disruption. The Outcomes for Children*. London: Family Policy Studies Centre.

Burke, K.C., Burke, J.D. Jr., Regier, D.A. and Rae, D.S. (1990) 'Age at the onset of select mental disorders in five community populations', *Archive of General Psychiatry*, 5: 511–18.

Burnhill, P., Garner, C. and McPherson, A. (1990) 'Parental education, social class and entry into higher education 1976–86', *Journal of the Royal Statistical Society*, Series A, 153: 233–48.

Burr, A. (1989) 'An inner city community response to heroin use', in S. MacGregor (ed.) *Drugs and British Society*. London: Routledge.

Butler, D. and Kavanagh, D. (1992) *The British General Election of 1992*. Basingstoke: Macmillan.

Button, E.J. and Whitehouse, A. (1981) 'Subclinical anorexia nervosa', *Psychological Medicine*, 11: 509–16.

Bynner, J. and Ashford, S. (1994) 'Politics and participation. Some antecedents of young people's attitudes to the political system and political activity', *European Journal of Social Psychology*, 24: 223–36.

Bynner, J. and Roberts, K. (eds) (1991) *Youth and Work. Transitions to Employment in England and Germany*. London: Anglo-German Foundation.

Bynner, J. and Steedman, J. (1995) *Basic Skills. Findings from the 1970 British Cohort Study*. London: Basic Skills Agency.

Campbell, A. (1981) *Girl Delinquents*. Oxford: Blackwell.

Campbell, B. (1993) *Goliath. Britain's Dangerous Places*. London: Methuen.

Carter, M.P. (1962) *Home, School and Work*. London: Pergamon.

Carvel, J. (1996) 'Third of boys aged 15 carry arms'. *The Guardian*, 15 May.

Cashmore, E.E. (1984) *No Future. Youth and Society*. London: Heinemann.

Central Statistical Office (CSO) (1972) *Social Trends*, 3. London: HMSO.

Central Statistical Office (CSO) (1994) *Social Trends*, 24. London: HMSO.

Central Statistical Office (CSO) (1995a) *Social Trends*, 25. London: HMSO.

Central Statistical Office (CSO) (1995b) *Regional Trends*, 30. London: HMSO.

Central Statistical Office (CSO) (1996) *Social Trends*, 26. London: HMSO.

Chernin, K. (1986) *Womansize. The Tyranny of Slenderness*. London: Woman's Press.

Chisholm, L., Büchner, P., Krüger, H.-H. and Brown, P. (1990) 'Childhood and youth in the United Kingdom and West Germany. An introduction', in L. Chisholm, P. Büchner, H.-H. Krüger and P. Brown (eds) *Childhood, Youth and Social Change. A Comparative Perspective*. London: Falmer.

Chitty, C. (ed.) (1987) *Aspects of Vocationalism*. London: Institute of Post-16 Education.

Chitty, C. (1989) *Towards a New Educational System. The Victory of the New Right?* London: Falmer.

Clarke, C. and Critcher, C. (1985) *The Devil Makes Work. Leisure in Capitalist Britain*. Basingstoke: Macmillan.

Clough, E., Gray, J., Jones, B. and Pattie, C. (1986) *Routes Through YTS*. Youth Cohort Studies No. 2. Sheffield: Manpower Services Commission.

Coakley, J. and White, A. (1992) 'Making decisions: Gender and sport participation among British adolescents', *Sociology of Sport Journal*, 9: 20–35.

Cochrane, R. and Billig, M. (1982) 'Adolescent support for the National Front', *New Community*, 10: 86–94.

Cochrane, R. and Billig, M. (1983) 'Youth and politics in the 80s', *Youth and Policy*, 2: 31–4.

Cockburn, C. (1987) *Two Track Training. Sex Inequalities and the YTS*. Basingstoke: Macmillan.

Coffield, F., Borrill, C. and Marshall, S. (1986) *Growing up at the Margins*. Milton Keynes: Open University Press.

Cohen, J. (1983) 'Rethinking social movements', *Berkeley Journal of Sociology*, 28: 97–113.

Cohen, S. (1972) *Folk Devils and Moral Panics*. Oxford: Blackwell.

Colby, A. and Kohlberg, L. (1987) *The Measurement of Moral Judgement. Vol.1. Theoretical Foundations*. Cambridge: Cambridge University Press.

Coleman, J. and Husen, T. (1985) *Becoming an Adult in a Changing Society*. Paris: OECD.

Coleman, C. and Moynihan, J. (1996) *Understanding Crime Data. Haunted by the Dark Figure*. Buckingham: Open University Press.

Coles, B. (1995) *Youth and Social Policy*. London: University College London.

Côté, J.E. and Allahar, A.L. (1996) *Generation on Hold. Coming of Age in the Late Twentieth Century*. New York: New York University Press.

Courtenay, G. (1988) *England and Wales Youth Cohort Study. Report on Cohort 1, Sweep 1*. Sheffield: Manpower Services Commission.

Courtenay, G. and McAleese, I. (1993) *England and Wales Youth Cohort Study. Report on Cohort 5, Sweep 1*. Sheffield: Employment Department.

Craig, G. (1991) *Fit for Nothing? Young People, Benefits and Youth Training*. London: The Children's Society.

Crompton, R. (1992) 'Where did all the bright girls go? Women's higher education and employment since 1964', in N. Abercrombie and A. Warde (eds) *Social Change in Contemporary Britain*. Oxford: Polity.

Cross, M., Wrench, J. and Barnett, S. (1990) *Ethnic Minorities and the Careers Service. An Investigation into Processes of Assessment and Placement*. London: Department of Employment.

D'Attilio, J.P., Campbell, B.M., Lubold, P., Jacobson, T. and Richard, J. A. (1992) 'Social support and suicide potential: Preliminary findings for adolescent populations', *Psychological Reports*, 70: 76–8.

DaVanzo, J. and Goldscheider, F.K. (1990) 'Coming home again. Returns to the family home of young adults', *Population Studies*, 44: 241–55.

Davies, J.B. and Stacey, B. (1972) *Teenagers and Alcohol*. London: HMSO.

Davis, J. (1990) *Youth and the Condition of Britain. Images of Adolescent Conflict*. London: Athlone.

Deakin, B.M (1996) *The Youth Labour Market in Britain. The Role of Intervention*. Cambridge: Cambridge University Press.

DEE (1995) *Labour Market Quarterly Report*, November. London: Department of Employment.

Deem, R. (1986) *All Work and No Play. The Sociology of Women and Leisure*. Milton Keynes: Open University Press.

Delamont, S. (1980) *Sex Roles and the School*. London: Methuen.

Dennis, N., Henriques, F. and Slaughter, C. (1956) *Coal is Our Life*. London: Eyre and Spottiswoode.

Department for Education (DFE) (1993) 'International statistical comparisons of the participation in education and training of 16 to 18-year-olds', *Statistical Bulletin*, 19/93, London: HMSO.

Department for Education (DFE) (1994a) *Statistical Bulletin*, 13/94. London: HMSO.

Department for Education (DFE) (1994b) *Statistical Bulletin*, 1/94. London: HMSO.

Department for Education (DFE) (1994c) *Statistical Bulletin*, 10/94. London: HMSO.

Department for Education and Employment (DfEE) (1994) *Employment Gazette*, 102. London: HMSO.

Department for Education and Employment (DfEE) (1995) *Employment Gazette*, 103. London: HMSO.

Department for Education and Employment (DfEE) (1996) *Labour Market Trends*, 104. London: HMSO.

Department of Education and Science (DES) (1985) *Statistical Bulletin*, 5/85. London: HMSO.

Department of Employment (1994) *Labour Market and Skill Trends. 1995/96*. London: Department for Employment.

de Wilde, E.J., Kienhorst, C.W.M., Diekstra, R.F.W. and Wolters, W.H.G. (1992) 'The relationship between adolescent suicidal behaviour and life events in childhood and adolescence', *American Journal of Psychiatry*, 1: 45–51.

Dex, S. (1985) *The Sexual Division of Work. Conceptual Revolution in the Social Sciences*. Brighton: Wheatsheaf.

Diekstra, R.F.W., Garnefski, N., Heus, P. de, Zwart, R. de, Praag, B. van, and Warnaar, M. (1991) *Scholierenonderzoek 1990. Gedrag en gezondheid*. Den Haag: NIBUD.

Diekstra, R.F.W., Kienhorst, C.W.M. and de Wilde, E.J. (1995) 'Suicide and suicidal behaviours among adolescents', in M. Rutter and D.J. Smith (eds) *Psychological Disorders in Young People. Time Trends and their Causes*. Chichester: John Wiley and Sons.

Donoghue, B. (1992) *The Time of Your Life? The Truth About Being Young in 90s Britain*. London: British Youth Council.

Donovan, C. (1990) 'Adolescent sexuality', *British Medical Journal*, 30: 1026–7.

Dore, R. (1976) *The Diploma Disease*. London: Allen and Unwin.

Douglas, J.W.B. (1967) *The Home and the School*. St Albans: Panther.

Douvan, A. and Adelson, J. (1966) *The Adolescent Experience*. New York: Wiley.

Downes, D. (1966) *The Delinquent Solution. A Study in Subcultural Theory*. London: Routledge and Kegan Paul.

Drew, D., Gray, J. and Sime, N. (1992) *Against the Odds. The Education and Labour Market Experiences of Black Young People*. Sheffield: Employment Department.

Driscoll, M. and Kelly, F. (1996) 'Party people', *Sunday Times*, 18 February.

Dunnell, K. (1976) *Family Formation*. London: HMSO.

Durex (1990) *The Durex Report*. London: LRC Products Ltd.

Durkheim, E. (1947) *The Division of Labour in Society*. New York: Macmillan.

Durkheim, E. (1964) *The Rules of Sociological Method*. New York: Free Press.

Egerton, M. and Halsey, A.H. (1993) 'Trends in social class and gender in access to higher education in Britain', *Oxford Review of Education*, 19: 183–96.

Elias, N. (1978) *The History of Manners. The Civilising Process*, Volume I. Oxford: Blackwell.

Elias, N. (1982) *State Formation and Civilisation. The Civilising Process*, Volume II. Oxford: Blackwell.

Emler, N. (1996) 'A new agenda for youth politics research? The contribution of a social psychological perspective', conference paper, University of Glasgow, British Youth Research: The New Agenda, 26–28 January.

Erikson, E.H. (1968) *Identity, Youth and Crisis*. New York: Norton.

Evans, K. and Furlong, A. (1997) 'Metaphors of youth transitions. Niches, pathways, trajectories or navigations', in J. Bynner, L. Chisholm and A. Furlong (eds) *Youth, Citizenship and Social Change in a European Context*. Aldershot: Avebury.

Farrell, G., Mansur, K. and Tullis, M. (1996) 'Cocaine and heroin in Europe', *British Journal of Criminology*, 36: 255–78.

Farrington, D.P. (1990) 'Implications of criminal career research for the prevention of offending', *Journal of Adolescence*, 13: 93–113.

Farrington, D., Gallagher, B., Morley, L., St Ledger, R. and West, D.J. (1986) 'Unemployment, school-leaving and crime', *British Journal of Criminology*, 26: 335–56.

Fay, R.E., Turner, C.F., Klassen, A.D. and Gagnon, J.H. (1989) 'Prevalance and patterns of some gender sexual contact among men', *Science*, 243: 338–48.

Fazey, C. (1991) 'The consequences of illegal drug use', in D. Whynes and P. Bean (eds) *Policing and Prescribing. The British System of Drug Control*. London: Macmillan.

Featherstone, M. (1991) *Consumer Culture and Postmodernism*. London: Sage.

Ferchoff, W. (1990) 'West German youth cultures at the close of the eighties', in L. Chisholm, P. Büchner, H.-H. Krüger and P. Brown (eds) *Childhood, Youth and Social Change. A Comparative Perspective*. Basingstoke: Falmer.

Feuer, L.S. (1969) *The Conflict of Generations. The Character and Significance of Student Movements*. New York: Basic Books.

Finch, J. (1989) *Family Obligations and Social Change*. Cambridge: Polity.

Fitzgerald, M. (1993) *The Royal Commission on Criminal Justice. Minorities and the Criminal Justice System*. London: HMSO.

Fogelman, K. (1996) 'Citizenship education', conference paper, University of Glasgow, British Youth Research: The New Agenda, 26–28 January.

Fombonne, E. (1995) 'Eating disorders. Time trends and possible exploratory mechanisms', in M. Rutter and D.J. Smith (eds) *Psychological Disorders in Young People. Time Trends and Their Causes*. Chichester: Wiley.

Ford, J. (1969) *Social Class and the Comprehensive School*. London: Routledge and Kegan Paul.

Ford, N. and Morgan, K. (1989) 'Heterosexual lifestyles of young people in an English city', *Journal of Population and Social Studies*, 1: 38–48.

Foreman, D. and Chilvers, C. (1989) 'Sexual behaviour of young and middle aged men in England and Wales', *British Medical Journal*, 298: 1137–42.

Fossey, E., Loretto, W. and Plant, M. (1996) 'Alcohol and youth', in L. Harrison (ed.) *Alcohol Problems in the Community*. London: Routledge.

Foster, K., Wilmot, A. and Dobbs, J. (1990) *General Household Survey 1988*. London: HMSO.

Franklin, M.N. (1985) *The Decline in Class Voting in Britain*. Oxford: Clarendon.

Frith, S. (1978) *The Sociology of Rock*. Constable: London.

Fryer, D. and Payne, R. (1986) 'Being unemployed. A review of the literature on the psychosocial experience of unemployment', in C.L. Cooper and I. Robertson (eds) *International Review of Industrial and Organisational Psychology*. Chichester: Wiley.

Furlong, A. (1992) *Growing Up in a Classless Society*. Edinburgh: Edinburgh University Press.

Furlong, A. (1993) 'The youth transition, unemployment and labour market disadvantage. Gambling on YTS', *Youth and Policy*, 41: 24–35.

Furlong, A., Campbell, R. and Roberts, K. (1990) 'The effects of post-16 experiences and social class on the leisure patterns of young adults', *Leisure Studies*, 9: 213–24.

Furlong, A. and Cooney, G. (1990) 'Getting on their bikes. Early home leaving among Scottish youth', *Journal of Social Policy*, 19: 535–51.

Furlong, A. and Raffe, D. (1989) *Young People's Routes into the Labour Market*. Edinburgh: Industry Department for Scotland.

Furlong, A. and Spearman, M. (1989) 'Psychological well-being and the transition from school', *British Journal of Education and Work*, 3: 49–55.

Furnham, A. and Gunter, B. (1983) 'Political knowledge and awareness in adolescence', *Journal of Adolescence*, 6: 385–400.

Furnham, A. and Gunter, B. (1989) *The Anatomy of Adolescence*. London: Routledge.

Furnham, A. and Stacey, B. (1991) *Young People's Understanding of Society*. London: Routledge.

Gallie, D. (1994) 'Are the unemployed an underclass? Some evidence from the social change and economic life initiative', *Sociology*, 28: 737–57.

Gallup/Wrangler (1992) *The Youth Report*. London: Gallup.

Garfinkel, P.E. and Garner, D.M. (1982) *Anorexia Nervosa. A Multidimensional Perspective*. New York: Brunner/Mazel.

Garner, C.L. and Raudenbush, S.W. (1991) 'Neighbourhood effects on educational attainment. A multi-level analysis', *Sociology of Education*, 64: 251–62.

Garton, A.F and Pratt, C. (1991) 'Leisure activities of adolescent school students. Predictors of participation and interest', *Journal of Adolescence*, 14: 305–21.

Gewirtz, S. (1996) 'Market discipline versus comprehensive education. A case study of a London comprehensive school struggling to survive in the education market place', in J. Ahier, B. Cosin and M. Hales (eds) *Diversity and Change. Education, Policy and Selection*. London: Routledge.

Giddens, A. (1990) *The Consequences of Modernity*. Oxford: Polity.

Giddens, A. (1991) *Modernity and Self Identity. Self and Society in the Late Modern Age*. Oxford: Polity.

Giggs, J. (1991) 'The epidemiology of contemporary drug abuse', in D. Whynes and P. Bean (eds) *Policing and Prescribing. The British System of Drug Control*. London: Macmillan.

Glendinning, A., Love, J.G., Hendry, L.B. and Shucksmith, J. (1992) 'Adolescence and health inequalities. Extensions to Macintyre and West', *Social Science Medicine*, 35: 679–87.

ster, H. (1995) *British Social Policy Since 1945*. Oxford: Blackwell.

S. (1989) *Leisure and Unemployment*. Milton Keynes: Open University Press.

────, E. (1991) *Drinking in England and Wales in the Late 1980s*. London: HMSO.

Goldscheider, F.K. and DaVanzo, J. (1986) 'Pathways to independent living in early adulthood. Marriage, semi-autonomy and pre-marital residential independence', *Demography*, 26: 597–614.

Goldscheider, F.K. and Goldscheider, C. (1993) *Leaving Home Before Marriage. Ethnicity, Familism, and Generational Relationships*. Madison, WI: University of Wisconsin Press.

Goldthorpe, J.H. and Marshall, G. (1992) 'The promising future of class analysis. A response to recent critiques', *Sociology*, 26: 381–400.

Gottfredson, M.R. and Hirschi, T. (1990) *A General Theory of Crime*. Stanford, CA: Stanford University Press.

Goudsblom, J. (1977) *Sociology in the Balance*. Oxford: Blackwell.

Graham, J. and Bowling, B. (1995) *Young People and Crime*. Home Office Research Study 145, London: Home Office.

Gratton, C. and Taylor, P. (1985) *Sports and Recreation. An Economic Evaluation*. London: Spon.

Gray, J., McPherson, A.F. and Raffe, D. (1983) *Reconstructions of Secondary Education. Theory, Myth and Practice Since the War*. London: Routledge and Kegan Paul.

Gray, J., Jesson, D. and Sime, N. (1992) 'The discouraged worker revisited. Post-16 participation in education south of the border', *Sociology*, 26: 493–505.

Green, E., Hebron, S. and Woodward, D. (1990) *Women's Leisure, What Leisure?* Basingstoke: Macmillan.

Green, F. (1989) 'Evaluating structural economic change. Britain in the 1980s', in F. Green (ed.) *The Restructuring of the UK Economy*. Hemel Hempstead: Harvester Wheatsheaf.

Green, G., Macintyre, S., West, P. and Ecob, R. (1991) 'Like parent like child? Associations between drinking and smoking behaviour of parents and their children', *British Journal of Addiction*, 86: 745–58.

Guardian (1995) 'Toon army reach fever pitch on the title trail', 25 August.

Gunter, B. (1987) *Television and Fear of Crime*. London: Libbey.

Hagan, J., Gillis, A.R. and Brownfield, D. (1996) (eds) *Criminological Controversies*. Oxford: Westview.

Hagell, A. and Newburn, T. (1994) *Persistent Young Offenders*. London: Policy Studies Institute.

Hakim, C. (1979) *Occupational Segregation. A Comparative Study of the Degree and Patterns of Differentiation Between Men's and Women's Work in Britain, the United States and Other Countries*. London: Department of Employment.

Hall, G.S. (1904) *Adolescence. Its Psychology and its Relations to Physiology, Anthropology, Sociology, Sex, Crime, Religion and Education*, 2 Vols., New York: Appleton.

Hall, S. and Jefferson, T. (eds) (1976) *Resistance Through Rituals. Youth Subcultures in Post-War Britain*. London: Hutchinson.

Hallsworth, S. (1994) Understanding new social movements, *Sociology Review*, 4: 7–10.

Halsey, A.H. (1992) *Opening Wide the Doors of Higher Education*, Briefing Paper No. 6. London: National Commission on Education.

Halsey, A.H., Heath, A.F. and Ridge, J.M. (1980) *Origins and Destinations. Family, Class and Education in Modern Britain*. Oxford: Clarendon.

Hammer, T. (1992) 'Unemployment and the use of drugs and alcohol among young people', *British Journal of Addiction*, 87: 1571–81.

Hammer, T. (forthcoming) 'History dependence in youth unemployment', *European Sociological Review*.

Hargreaves, D. (1967) *Social Relations in a Secondary School*. London: Routledge and Kegan Paul.

Harris, C. (1983) *The Family and Industrial Society*. London: Allen and Unwin.

Harris, N. (1990) 'Social security and the transition to adulthood', *Journal of Social Policy*, 17: 501–23.

Hartless, J.M., Ditton, J., Nair, G. and Philips, S. (1995) 'More sinned against than sinning. A study of young teenagers' experiences of crime', *British Journal of Criminology*, 35: 114–33.

Haskey, J. (1994) 'Step families and step children in Great Britain', *Population Trends*, 76: 5–30.

Haskey, J. and Kiernan, K.E. (1989) 'Cohabitation in Great Britain. Characteristics and estimated numbers of cohabiting partners', *Population Trends*, 58: 23–32.

Haw, S. (1985) *Drug Problems in Greater Glasgow*. London: Chamelion.

Health Education Authority (HEA) (1992) *Tomorrow's Young Adults. 9–15 Year-Olds Look at Alcohol, Drugs, Exercise and Smoking*. London: Health Education Authority.

Heath, A., Curtice, J., Jowell, R., Evans, G., Field, J. and Witherspoon, S. (1991) *Understanding Political Change. The British Voter 1964–1987*. Oxford: Pergamon.

Heath, A. and Topf, R. (1987) 'Political culture in social attitudes', in R. Jowell, S. Witherspoon and L. Brook (eds) *British Social Attitudes Survey. The 1987 Report*. Gower: Aldershot.

Hebdige, D. (1979) *Subculture. The Meaning of Style*. London: Methuen.

Hebdige, D. (1988) *Hiding in the Light*. London: Comedia.

Heinz, W. (1987) 'The transition from school to work in crisis. Coping with threatening unemployment', *Journal of Adolescent Research*, 2: 127–41.

Henderson, K.A. (1991) 'The contribution of feminism to an understanding of leisure constraints', *Journal of Leisure Research*, 23: 363–77.

Hendry, L. and Raymond, M. (1983) 'Youth unemployment and lifestyles. Some educational considerations', *Scottish Educational Review*, 15: 28–40.

Hendry, L., Shucksmith, J., Love, J.G. and Glendinning, A. (1993) *Young People's Leisure and Lifestyles*. London: Routledge.

Hess, L.E. (1995) 'Changing family patterns in Western Europe. Opportunity and risk factors for adolescent development', in M. Rutter and D.J. Smith (eds) *Psychological Disorders in Young People. Time Trends and their Causes*. Chichester: Wiley.

Hill, K. (1995) *The Long Sleep. Young People and Suicide*. London: Virago.

Himmelweit, H.T., Humphreys, P. and Jaeger, M. (1985) *How Voters Decide*. Milton Keynes: Open University Press.

Hobbs, D. (1989) *Doing the Business*. Oxford: Oxford University Press.

Hogan, D., Hao, L. and Parish, W. (1990) 'Race, kin networks and assistance to mother headed families', *Social Forces*, 68: 797–812.

Hollands, R. (1990) *The Long Transition*. Basingstoke: Macmillan.

Hollands, R. (1995) *Friday Night, Saturday Night. Youth Cultural Identification in the Post-Industrial City*. Newcastle: University of Newcastle.

Home Office (1993) *Information on the Criminal Justice System in England and Wales. Digest 2*. London: Home Office.

Home Office (1993c) *Probation Statistics England and Wales, 1992*. London: Home Office.

Home Office (1995) 'Statistics of drug seizures and offenders dealt with in the UK, 1994', *Statistical Bulletin*, 24/95. London: Home Office.

Horkheimer, M. and Adorno, T. (1972) *Dialectic of Enlightenment*. New York: Herder and Herder.

Horner, M.S. (1971) 'Femininity and successful achievement', in M.H. Garskof (ed.) *Roles Women Play*. San Diego, CA: Brooks Cole.

Hoskins, M., Sung, J. and Ashton, D.N. (1989) *Job Competition and the Entry to Work*, discussion paper no. 111. Leicester: Department of Economics, University of Leicester.

Hough, M. (1995) *Anxiety About Crime. Findings from the 1994 British Crime Survey,* Home Office Research Study 147. London: Home Office.

Howard League (1995) *Banged Up, Beaten Up, Cutting Up. Report of the Howard League Commission of Inquiry into Violence in Penal Institutions for Young People.* London: Howard League.

Hsu, L.K.G. (1990) 'Body image disturbance. Time to abandon the concept for eating disorders', *International Journal of Eating Disorders,* 10: 15–30.

Humphries, S. (1991) *The Secret World of Sex.* London: Sidgwick and Jackson.

Hurrelmann, K. (1990) 'Basic issues and problems of health in adolescence', in K. Hurrelmann and F. Lösel (eds) *Health Hazards in Adolescence.* Berlin: de Gruyter.

Inglehart, R. (1977) *The Silent Revolution. Changing Values and Political Styles Among Western Publics.* Princeton, NJ: Princeton University Press.

Inglehart, R. (1990) *Culture Shift in Advanced Industrial Society.* Princeton, NJ: Princeton University Press.

Institute for Public Policy Research (IPPR) (1990) *A British 'Baccalaureate'. Ending the Division Between Education and Training.* London: Institute for Public Policy Research.

Irwin, S. (1995) 'Social reproduction and change in the transition from youth to adulthood', *Sociology,* 29: 293–315.

Jack, M.S. (1989) 'Personal fable. A potential explanation for risk-taking behaviour in adolescents', *Journal of Paediatric Nursing,* 4: 334–8.

Jackson, J.S. III (1973) 'Alienation and black participation', *Journal of Politics,* 35: 849–85.

Jacobs, J. (1971) *Adolescent Suicide.* London: Wiley Interscience.

Jansen, T. and Van der Veen, R. (1992) 'Reflexive modernity, self-reflexive biographies. Adult education in the light of the risk society', *International Journal of Lifelong Learning,* 11: 275–86.

Jessop, B., Bonnett, K., Bromley, S. and Ling, T. (1987) 'Popular capitalism, flexible accumulation and left strategy', *New Left Review,* 165: 104–22.

Johnson, A.M., Wadsworth, J., Elliot, P., Prior, L., Wallace, P., Blower, S., Webb, N.L., Heald, G.I., Miller, D.L., Adler, M.W. and Anderson, R.M. (1989) 'A pilot study of sexual lifestyles in a random sample of the population of Great Britain', *AIDS,* 3: 135–41.

Jones, D.J., Fox, M.M., Babigian, H.M. and Hutton, H.E. (1980) 'Epidemiology of anorexia nervosa in Munroe County, New York. 1960–1976', *Psychosomatic Medicine,* 42: 551–8.

Jones, G. (1987) 'Leaving the parental home. An analysis of early housing careers', *Social Policy,* 16: 49–74.

Jones, G. (1995) *Leaving Home.* Buckingham: Open University Press.

Jones, G. and Wallace, C. (1990) 'Beyond individualization. What sort of social change', in L. Chisholm, P. Büchner, H.-H. Krüger and P. Brown (eds) *Childhood, Youth and Social Change. A Comparative Perspective.* London: Falmer.

Jones, G. and Wallace, C. (1992) *Youth, Family and Citizenship.* Buckingham: Open University Press.

Kasl, S.V., Gore, S. and Cobb, S. (1975) 'The experience of losing a job. Reported changes in health, symptoms and illness behaviour', *Psychosomatic Medicine,* 37: 106–22.

Kaufman, L. (1980) 'Prime-time nutrition', *Journal of Communication,* summer: 37–46.

Kellner, D. (1992) 'Popular culture and the construction of postmodern identity', in S. Lash and J. Friedman (eds) *Modernity and Identity.* Oxford: Blackwell.

Kerckhoff, A.C. (1990) *Getting Started. Transition to Adulthood in Great Britain*. Oxford: Westview.

Kerckhoff, A.C. and McRae, J. (1992) 'Leaving the parental home in Great Britain. A comparative perspective', *Sociological Quarterly*, 33: 281–301.

Kiernan, K.E. (1985) *A Demographic Analysis of First Marriages in England and Wales. 1950–1985*, CPS Research Paper 85–1. London: Centre for Population Studies.

Kiernan, K.E . (1986) 'Leaving home. A comparative analysis of six western European countries', *European Journal of Population*, 2: 177–84.

Kiernan, K.E. (1992) 'The impact of family disruption in childhood on transitions made in young adult life', *Population Studies*, 46: 213–34.

Kiernan, K.E. and Estaugh, V. (1993) *Cohabitation. Extra-Marital Childbearing and Social Policy*. London: Family Studies Policy Centre.

Krahn, H. J. and Lowe, G. S. (1993) *Work, Industry and Canadian Society*. Scarborough, Ontario: Nelson.

Kreitman, N. (1977) *Parasuicide*. London: Wiley.

Krüger, H.-H. (1990) 'Caught between homogenization and disintegration, changes in the life-phase. "Youth" in West Germany since 1945', in L. Chisholm, P. Büchner, H.-H. Krüger and P. Brown (eds) *Childhood, Youth and Social Change. A Comparative Perspective*. Basingstoke: Falmer.

Kumar, K. (1995) *From Post-Industrial to Post-Modern Society*. Oxford: Blackwell.

Kutcher, S. (1994) 'Adolescence. Normal development and some important psychiatric conditions onsetting in the teenage years', in R.S. Tonkin (ed.) *Current Issues in the Adolescent Patient*. London: Baillière Tindall.

Lader, D. and Matheson, J. (1991) *Smoking Among Secondary School Children in 1990*. London: OPCS.

Langman, L. (1992) 'Neon cages. Shopping for subjectivity', in R. Shields (ed.) *Shopping. The Subject of Consumption*. London: Routledge.

Lash, S. (1992) *Modernity and Identity*. Oxford: Blackwell.

Lash, S. and Urry, J. (1987) *The End of Organised Capital*. Cambridge: Polity.

Layard, R., Mayhew, L. and Owen, G. (1994) *Britain's Training Deficit*. Aldershot: Avebury.

Lea, J. and Young, J. (1993) *What Is to Be Done About Law and Order? Crisis in the Nineties*. London: Pluto.

Lee, D., Marsden, D., Rickman, P. and Duncombe, J. (1990) *Scheming for Youth. A Study of YTS in the Enterprise Culture*. Milton Keynes: Open University Press.

Leitner, M., Shapland, J. and Wiles, P. (1993) *Drug Usage and Prevention. The Views and Habits of the General Public*. London: HMSO.

Leonard, D. (1980) *Sex and Generation. A Study of Courtship and Weddings*. London: Tavistock.

Lichtman, R. (1970) 'Symbolic interactionism and social reality. Some Marxist queries', *Berkeley Journal of Sociology*, 15: 75–94.

Lister Sharp, D. (1994) 'Underage drinking in the United Kingdom since 1970. Public policy, the law and adolescent drinking behaviour', *Alcohol and Alcoholism*, 29: 5–63.

Littlewood, P. and Jönsson, I. (1996) 'European schooling and social justice. Some current trends', in A. Erskine, M. Elchardus, S. Herkommer and J. Ryan (eds) *Changing Europe. Some Aspects of Identity, Conflict and Social Justice*. Aldershot: Avebury.

Lowden, S. (1989) *Three Years On. The Reaction of Young People to Scotland's Action Plan*. Edinburgh: Centre for Educational Sociology, University of Edinburgh.

Lucey, H. (1996) 'Transitions to womanhood. Constructions of success and failure for middle and working class young women', conference paper, University of Glasgow, British Youth Research: The New Agenda, 26–28 January.

Lyon, J. (1996) Adolescents who offend, *Journal of Adolescence*, 19: 1–4.

Lyotard, J.-F. (1984) *The Postmodern Condition. A Report on Knowledge.* Minneapolis, MN: University of Minnesota Press.

MacDonald, R. (1996) 'Youth transitions at the margins', conference paper, University of Glasgow, British Youth Research: The New Agenda, 26–28 January.

MacDonald, R. and Coffield, F. (1991) *Risky Business? Youth and the Enterprise Culture.* London: Falmer.

Macintyre, S. (1988) 'Social correlates of human height', *Science Progress Oxford*, 72: 493–510.

McPherson, A.F. and Willms, J.D. (1987) 'Equalisation and improvement. Some effects of comprehensive re-organisation in Scotland', *Sociology*, 21: 509–39.

McQuoid, J. (1996) 'The ISRD study. Self report findings from Northern Ireland', *Journal of Adolescence*, 19: 95–8.

McRae, S. (1987) 'Social and political perspectives found among young unemployed men and women', in M. White (ed.) *The Social World of the Young Unemployed.* London: Policy Studies Institute.

McRobbie, A. (1993) 'Shut up and dance. Youth culture and changing modes of femininity', *Cultural Studies*, 7: 406–26.

Maguire, M. (1991) 'British labour market trends', in D.N. Ashton and G. Lowe (eds) *Making Their Way. Education, Training and the Labour Market in Canada and Britain.* Milton Keynes: Open University Press.

Mann, A.H., Wakeling, A., Wood, K., Monck, E., Dobbs, R. and Szmakler, G. (1983) 'Screening for abnormal eating attitudes and psychiatric morbidity in an unselected population of 15 year old schoolgirls', *Psychological Medicine*, 13: 573–88.

Marsh, A. (1990) *Political Action in Europe and the USA.* London: Macmillan.

Marsh, A., Dobbs, J. and White, A. (1986) *Adolescent Drinking.* London: HMSO.

Marshall, G. and Swift, A. (1993) 'Social class and social justice', *British Journal of Sociology*, 44: 187–211.

Martin, J. and Roberts, C. (1984) *Women and Work. A Lifetime Perspective.* London: HMSO.

Maung, N. (1995) *Young People, Victimisation and the Police. British Crime Survey Findings on Experiences and Attitudes of 12 to 15 Year Olds*, Home Office Research Study 140. London: HMSO.

May, C. and Cooper, A. (1995) 'Personal identity and social change. Some theoretical considerations', *Acta Sociologica*, 38: 75–85.

Mays, J.B. (1954) *Growing Up in the City. A Study of Juvenile Delinquency in an Urban Neighbourhood.* Liverpool: Liverpool University Press.

Meadows, G.N., Palmer, R.L., Newball, E.U.M. and Kendrick, J.M.T. (1986) 'Eating attitudes and disorder in young women. A general practice based survey', *Psychological Medicine*, 16: 351–7.

Measham, F., Newcombe, R. and Parker, H. (1994) 'The normalisation of recreational drug use amongst young people in north-west England', *British Journal of Sociology*, 45: 287–312.

Meeus, W. (1994) 'Psychosocial problems and support', in F. Nestmann and K. Hurrelmann (eds) *Social Networks and Social Support in Childhood and Adolescence.* Berlin: de Gruyter.

Melucci, A. (1992) 'Youth silence and voice. Selfhood and commitment in the everyday experiences of adolescents', in Fornas, J. and Bolin, G. (eds) *Moves in Modernity.* Stockholm: Almqvist and Wiskell.

Mennell, S., Murcott, A. and van Otterloo, A.H. (1992) *The Sociology of Food. Eating, Diet and Culture.* London: Sage.

Merton, R.K. (1969) 'Social structure and anomie', in D.R. Cressey and D.A. Ward (eds) *Delinquency, Crime and Social Processes.* New York: Harper and Row.

Messerschmidt, J. W. (1994) 'Schooling, masculinities and youth crime', in T. Newburn and E.A. Stanko (eds) *Just Boys Doing the Business? Men, Masculinities and Crime*. London: Routledge.

Miles, R. (1982) *Racism and Migrant Labour. A Critical Text*. London: Routledge.

Miles, R. (1989) *Racism*. London: Routledge.

Miles, S. (1995) 'Pleasure or pressure. Consumption and youth identity in the contemporary British shopping centre', conference paper, University of Leicester, British Sociological Association, 10–13 April.

Miles, S. (1996) 'Use and consumption in the construction of identities', conference paper, University of Glasgow, British Youth Research: The New Agenda, 26–28 January.

Minuchin, S. (1978) *Psychosomatic Families. Anorexia Nervosa in Context*. Cambridge, MA: Harvard University Press.

Mizen, P. (1995) *The State, Young People and Youth Training. In and Against the Training State*. London: Mansell.

Moon, B. (1995) 'Let's raise our glasses', *Guardian Education*, 11 July.

Mott, J. (1985) 'Self-reported cannabis use in Great Britain in 1981', *British Journal of Addiction*, 80: 37–43.

Mott, J. (1991) 'Crime and heroin use', in D. Whynes and P. Bean (eds) *Policing and Prescribing. The British System of Drug Control*. London: Macmillan.

Mott, J. and Mirrless-Black, C. (1993) *Self-Reported Drug Misuse in England and Wales. Main Findings from the 1992 British Crime Survey*. London: Home Office.

Mowl, G. and Towner, J. (1994) 'Same city, different worlds? Women's leisure in two areas of Tyneside', in I. Henry (ed.) *Leisure. Modernity, Postmodernity and Lifestyles*. Leeds: Leisure Studies Association.

Muncie, J. and McLaughlin, E. (1995) *The Problem of Crime*. London: Sage.

Murdock, G. and McCron, R. (1976) 'Youth and class. The career of a confusion', in G. Mungham and G. Pearson (eds) *Working Class Youth Culture*. London: Routledge and Kegan Paul.

Murray, C. (1990) *The Emerging British Underclass*. London: Institute of Economic Affairs.

Murray, I. (1996) 'Jobseeker's Allowance. Cuts to benefit and transitional arrangements', *Unemployment Unit Working Brief*, 73: 9–13.

Nee, C. (1993) *Car Theft. The Offender's Perspective*. London: Home Office.

Newburn, T. and Stanko, E.A. (1994) 'Introduction. Men, masculinities and crime', in T. Newburn and E. A. Stanko (eds) *Just Boys Doing the Business? Men, Masculinities and Crime*. London: Routledge.

Newcombe, R. (1987) 'High time for harm reduction', *Druglink*, 2: 10–11.

O'Bryan, L. (1989) 'Young people and drugs', in S. MacGregor (ed.) *Drugs and British Society*. London: Routledge.

Offer, D., Ostrov, E., Howard, K. and Atkinson, R. (1988) *The Teenage World*. New York: Plenum.

Office of Population Censuses and Surveys (OPCS) (1995) *General Household Survey, 1993*. London. HMSO.

Ohri, S. and Faruqi, S. (1988) 'Racism, employment and unemployment', in A. Bhat, R. Carr-Hill and S. Ohri (eds) *Britain's Black Population. A New Perspective*. Aldershot: Gower.

O'Reilly, K.R. and Aral, S.O. (1985) 'Adolescent and sexual behaviour', *Journal of Adolescent Health Care*, 6: 262–70.

Organization for Economic Cooperation and Development (OECD) (1995) *Education at a Glance*, 3rd edn. Paris: OECD.

Pahl, R.E. (1989) 'Is the emperor naked? Some comments on the adequacy of sociological theory in urban and regional research', *International Journal of Urban and Regional Research*, 15: 127–9.

Pahl R.E. (1993) 'Does class analysis without class theory have a promising future?' *Sociology*, 27: 253–8.

Park, A. (1994) *England and Wales Youth Cohort Study Cohort 4. Young people 18–19 years old in 1991. Report on Sweep 3.* London: Employment Department.

Park, A. (1996) 'Teenagers and their politics', in R. Jowell, J. Curtice, A. Park, L. Brook and D. Ahrendt (eds) *British Social Attitudes Survey. 12th Report.* Dartmouth: Aldershot.

Parker, H.J. (1974) *View From the Boys.* Newton Abbot: David and Charles.

Parker, H., Bakx, K. and Newcombe, R. (1987) 'The new heroin users. Prevalence and characteristics in Wirral, Merseyside', *British Journal of Addiction*, 82: 147–58.

Parker, H., Bakx, K. and Newcombe, R. (1988) *Living with Heroin.* Milton Keynes: Open University Press.

Parker, H. and Newcombe, R. (1987) 'Heroin use and acquisitive crime in an English community', *British Journal of Sociology*, 38: 329–50.

Parry-Jones, W.L.I. (1988) 'Obesity in children and adolescence', in G.B. Burrows, P. Beumont and R.C. Casper (eds) *Handbook of Eating Disorders. Part 2, Obesity.* Amsterdam: Elsevier.

Paterson, L. (1992) 'The influence of opportunity on aspirations among prospective university entrants from Scottish schools', *Journal of the Royal Statistical Society (Series A)*, 155: 37–60.

Paterson, L. and Raffe, D. (1995) 'Staying-on in full-time education in Scotland. 1985–1991', *Oxford Review of Education*, 21: 3–23.

Payne, J. (1995) *Routes Beyond Compulsory Schooling*, Youth Cohort Paper No. 31. London: Employment Department.

Pearson, G. (1983) *Hooligan. A History of Respectable Fears.* Basingstoke: Macmillan.

Pearson, G. (1987) *The New Heroin Users.* Oxford: Blackwell.

Pearson, G. (1994) 'Youth, crime and society', in M. Maguire, R. Morgan and R. Reiner (eds) *The Oxford Handbook of Criminology.* Oxford: Clarendon.

Pearson, G., Gilman, M. and McIver, S. (1987) *Young People and Heroin Use in the North of England.* London: Gower.

Peck, D.F. and Plant, M.A. (1986) 'Unemployment and illegal drug use. Concordant evidence from a prospective study and from national trends', *British Medical Journal*, 293: 929–32.

Penhale, B. (1990) *Living Arrangements of Young Adults in France, England and Wales*, LS Working Paper 68. London: Social Statistics Research Unit, City University.

Plant, M.A. (1989) 'The epidemiology of illicit drug-use and misuse in Britain', in S. MacGregor (ed.) *Drugs and British Society.* London: Routledge.

Plant, M.A., Bagnall, G., Foster, J. and Sales, E. (1991) Young people and drinking. Results of an English national survey, *Alcohol and Alcoholism*, 25: 685–90.

Plant, M.A. and Foster, J. (1991) 'Teenagers and alcohol. Results of a Scottish national survey', *Drug and Alcohol Dependence*, 28: 203–10.

Plant, M. A., Peck, D. F. and Samuel, E. (1985) *Alcohol, Drugs and School Leavers.* London: Tavistock.

Plant, M. A. and Plant, M. (1992) *Risk-Takers. Alcohol, Drugs, Sex and Youth.* London: Routledge.

Platt, S. and Kreitman, N. (1990) 'Long term trends in parasuicide in Edinburgh, 1968–87', *Social Psychiatry and Psychiatric Epidemiology*, 25: 56–61.

Poole, M. E. (1989) 'Adolescent transitions. A life-course perspective', in K. Hurrelman and U. Engel (eds) *The Social World of Adolescents. International Perspectives.* Berlin: de Gruyter.

Pryce, K. (1979) *Endless Pressure: A Study of West Indian Lifestyles in Bristol.* Harmondsworth: Penguin.

Raffe, D. (1989) 'Longitudinal and historical changes in young people's attitudes to YTS', *British Educational Research Journal*, 15: 129–39.

Raffe, D. (1990) 'The transition from school to work. Content, context and the external labour market', in C. Wallace and M. Cross (eds) *Youth in Transition. The Sociology of Youth and Youth Policy.* London: Falmer.

Raffe, D. (1992) *Participation of 16–19 Year-Olds in Education and Training,* Briefing Paper No. 3. London: National Commission on Education.

Raffe, D. and Smith, P. (1987) 'Young people's attitudes to YTS. The first two years', *British Educational Research Journal,* 13: 241–60.

Raffe, D. and Willms, J.D. (1989) 'Schooling the discouraged worker. Local labour-market effects on educational participation', *Sociology,* 23: 559–81.

Rapoport, R. and Rapoport, R.N. (1975) *Leisure and the Family Life-Cycle.* London: Routledge.

Reimer, B. (1995) 'Youth and modern lifestyles', in J. Fornas and G. Bolin (eds) *Youth Culture in Late Modernity.* London: Sage.

Rindfuss, R.R., Swicegood, C.G. and Rosenfeld, R.A. (1987) 'Disorder in the life course. How common and does it matter?' *American Sociological Review,* 52: 785–801.

Roberts, K. (1968) 'The entry into employment. An approach towards a general theory', *Sociological Review,* 16: 165–84.

Roberts, K. (1983) *Youth and Leisure.* London: Allen and Unwin.

Roberts, K. (1985) 'Youth in the 1980s: A new way of life', *International Social Science Journal,* 37: 427–40.

Roberts, K. (1995) *Youth and Employment in Modern Britain.* Oxford: Oxford University Press.

Roberts, K., Brodie, D.A., Campbell, R., Lamb, K., Minten, J. and York, C. (1989) 'Indoor sports centres. Trends in provision and usage', in Health Promotion Research Trust (ed.) *Fit for Life.* London: Health Promotion Research Trust.

Roberts, K., Campbell, C. and Furlong, A. (1990) 'Class and gender divisions among young people at leisure', in C. Wallace and M. Cross (eds) *Youth in Transition.* London: Falmer.

Roberts, K., Clark, S.C. and Wallace, C. (1994) 'Flexibility and individualisation. A comparison of transitions into employment in England and Germany', *Sociology,* 28: 31–54.

Roberts, K., Dench, S. and Richardson, D. (1987) *The Changing Structure of Youth Labour Markets.* London: Department of Employment.

Roberts, K. and Parsell, G. (1990) 'The political orientations, interests and activities of Britain's 16 to 18 year olds in the late 1980s', ESRC 16–19 Initiative Occasional Papers, No. 26. London: City University.

Roberts, K. and Parsell, G. (1992a) 'Entering the labour market in Britain. The survival of traditional opportunity structures', *Sociological Review,* 30: 727–53.

Roberts, K. and Parsell, G. (1992b) 'The stratification of youth training', *British Journal of Education and Work,* 5: 65–83.

Roberts, K. and Parsell, G. (1994) 'Youth cultures in Britain. The middle class take-over', *Leisure Studies,* 13: 33–48.

Rojek, C. (1985) *Capitalism and Leisure Theory.* London: Tavistock.

Rose, M. (1996) 'Still life in Swindon. Case-studies in union survival and employer policy in a 'Sunrise' labour market', in D. Gallie, R. Penn and M. Rose (eds) *Trade Unionism in Recession.* Oxford: Oxford University Press.

Rubenstein, D. (1981) *Marx and Wittgenstein. Social Praxis and Social Explanation.* London: Routledge and Kegan Paul.

Rudat, K., Ryan, H. and Speed, M. (1992) *Today's Young Adults. An In-depth Study into the Lifestyles of 16 to 19 Year Olds.* London: Health Education Authority.

Rüdig, W., Bennie, L. and Franklin, M. (1991) *Green Party Members. A Profile.* Glasgow: Delta Publications.

Runciman, W.G. (1966) *Relative Deprivation and Social Justice.* Berkeley, CA: University of California Press.

Russell, K. (1993) 'Lysergia suburbia', in S. Readhead (ed.) *Rave Off. Politics and Deviance in Contemporary Youth Culture.* Aldershot: Avebury.

Rutherford, A. (1992) *Growing Out of Crime. The New Era.* London: Waterside Press.

Rutter, M. and Smith, D.J. (eds) (1995) *Psychosocial Disorders in Young People. Time Trends and their Causes.* Chichester: Wiley.

Ryan, J. (1996) 'Gender, individualism and social change in Europe', in A. Erskine, M. Elchardus, S. Herkommer and J. Ryan (eds) *Changing Europe. Some Aspects of Identity, Conflict and Social Justice.* Aldershot: Avebury.

Sampson, R.J. and Laub, J.H. (1993) *Crime in the Making. Pathways and Turning Points Through Life.* Cambridge, MA: Harvard University Press.

Sanders, D. (1992) 'Why the Conservative Party won – again', in A. King, I. Crewe, D. Denver, K. Newton, P. Norton, D. Sanders and P. Seyd (eds) *Britain at the Polls, 1992.* Chatham, NJ: Chatham House Publishers Inc.

Savage, M. and Warde, A. (1993) *Urban Sociology, Capitalism and Modernity.* London: Macmillan.

Scarbrough, E. (1995) 'Materialist-postmaterialist value orientations', in J.W. Van Deth and E. Scarbrough (eds) *Beliefs in Government Volume Four. The Impact of Values.* New York: Oxford University Press.

Scarman, The Rt. Hon. The Lord (1981) *The Brixton Disorders,* Cmnd 8427. London: HMSO.

Schostak, J.F. (1983) 'Race, riots and unemployment', in R. Fiddy (ed.) *In Place of Work.* London: Falmer.

Scott, A. (1990) *Ideology and the New Social Movements.* London: Unwin Hyman.

Scottish Community Education Council (SCEC) (1994) *Being Young in Scotland.* Edinburgh: Scottish Community Education Council.

Scottish Health Service (1996) Estimates based on unpublished statistics from the Information Services Division.

Seabrook, J. (1983) *Unemployment.* London: Granada.

Selzer, V.L., Rabin, J. and Benjamin, F. (1989) 'Teenagers' awareness of acquired immunodeficiency syndrome and the impact on their sexual behaviour', *Obstetrics and Gynaecology,* 74: 55–8.

Sewell, W.H., Haller, A.O. and Strauss, M.A. (1957) 'Social status and educational and occupational aspirations', *American Sociological Review,* 22: 67–73.

Sewell, W.H. and Hauser, R.M. (1993) 'A review of the Wisconsin longitudinal study of social and psychological factors in aspirations and achievements. 1963–1993', Working paper 92–1. University of Wisconsin-Madison: Centre for Demography and Ecology.

Shafii, M. (1989) 'Completed suicide in children and adolescents. Methods of psychological autopsy', in C.R. Pfeffer (ed.) *Suicide Among Youth. Perspectives on Risk Prevention.* Washington DC: American Psychiatric Press.

Shavit, Y. and Blossfeld, H.P. (1993) *Persistent Inequality.* Boulder, CO: Westview.

Shoemaker, D.J. (1990) *Theories of Delinquency. An Examination of Explanations of Delinquent Behaviour,* 2nd edn. Oxford: Oxford University Press.

Shover, N. (1985) *Ageing Criminals.* London: Sage.

Silbereisen, R.K., Robins, L. and Rutter, M. (1995) 'Secular trends in substance use. Concepts and data on the impact of social change on alcohol and drug abuse', in M. Rutter and D.J. Smith (eds) *Psychological Disorders in Young People. Time Trends and Their Causes.* Chichester: Wiley.

Skellington, R. and Morris, P. (1992) *'Race' in Britain. Today.* London: Sage.

Smith, D.J. (1995) 'Youth crime and conduct disorders. Trends, patterns and causal explanations', in M. Rutter and D. J. Smith (eds) *Psychological Disorders in Young People. Time Trends and Their Causes.* Chichester: Wiley.

Smith, D.J. and Rutter, M. (1995) 'Time trends in psychosocial disorders of youth', in

M. Rutter and D.J. Smith (eds) *Psychological Disorders in Young People. Time Trends and Their Causes*. Chichester: Wiley.

Smith, D.J. and Tomlinson, S. (1989) *The School Effect. A Study of Multi-racial Comprehensives*. London: Policy Studies Institute.

Smith, D.M. (1987) 'Some patterns of reported leisure behaviour of young people', *Youth and Society*, 18: 255–81.

Smithers, A. and Robinson, P. (1989) *Increasing Participation in Higher Education*. London: British Petroleum Educational Service.

Smithers, A. and Robinson, P. (1995) *Post-18 Education. Growth, Change, Prospect*. London: Council for Industry and Higher Education.

Sonenstein, F.L., Pleck, J.H. and Ku, L.C. (1989) 'Sexual activity, condom use and AIDS awareness among adolescent males', *Family Planning Perspectives*, 21: 152–8.

South, N. (1994) 'Drugs. Control, crime and criminological studies', in M. Maguire, R. Morgan and R. Reiner (eds) *The Oxford Handbook of Criminology*. Oxford: Clarendon.

Spilsbury, M., Hoskins, M., Ashton, D.N. and Maguire, M.J. (1987) 'A note on trade union membership patterns of young people', *British Journal of Industrial Relations*, 25: 267–74.

Spours, K. (1995) *Post-16 Education and Training. Statistical Trends*. London: Institute of Education, University of London.

Springhall, J. (1986) *Coming of Age. Adolescence in Britain 1860–1960*. Dublin: Gill and Macmillan.

Stewart, F. (1992) 'The adolescent as consumer', in J.C. Coleman and C. Warren-Anderson (eds) *Youth and Policy in the 1990s. The Way Forward*. London: Routledge.

Stimson, G. (1987) 'The war on heroin. British policy and the international trade in illicit drugs', in N. Dorn and N. South (eds) *A Land Fit for Heroin*. London: Macmillan.

Stradling, R. (1977) *The Political Awareness of School Leavers*. London: Hansard Society.

Sunday Times (1995) 'Angry young men', 2 April.

Surridge, P. and Raffe, D. (1995) *The Participation of 16–19 Year Olds in Education and Training. Recent Trends*, CES Briefing Paper No. 1. Edinburgh: University of Edinburgh.

Sutherland, E.H. (1949) *Principles of Criminology*. Chicago, IL: Lippincott.

Sweeting, H. (1995) 'Reversals of fortune? Sex differences in health in childhood and adolescence', *Social Science Medicine*, 40: 77–90.

Tajfel, H. and Turner, J.C. (1979) 'An integrative theory of intergroup conflict', in W.G. Austin and S. Worchel (eds) *The Social Psychology of Intergroup Relations*. Monterey, CA: Brooks-Cole.

Talbot, M. (1979) *Women and Leisure*. London: Sports Council/ SSRC.

Tarling, R. (1982) *Unemployment and Crime*, Research Bulletin No. 14. London: Home Office.

Taylor, I. (1996) 'Fear of crime, urban fortunes and suburban social movements. Some reflections from Manchester', *Sociology*, 30: 317–37.

The Times (1996) 'Parents bearing greater share of university fees', 6 July.

Times Educational Supplement (1989) 'A less than flattering spot', 29 January.

Times Higher Educational Supplement (1994) 'Youth training fails the grade, 2 September.

Tomlinson, A. (ed.) (1990) *Consumption, Identity and Style*. London: Routledge.

Touraine, A. (1985) 'An introduction to the study of social movements', *Social Research*, 52: 749–87.

Townsend, A. (1991) 'Services and local economic development, *Area*, 23: 309–17.

Townsend, P. and Davidson, N. (1982) *Inequalities in Health. The Black Report*. Harmondsworth: Penguin.

Wadsworth, M.E.J. and Maclean, M. (1986) 'Parents' divorce and children's life chances', *Children and Youth Services Review*, 8: 145–59.

Wallace, C. (1987) *For Richer, for Poorer. Growing up in and out of Work*. London: Tavistock.

Waller, P.J. (1981) 'The riots in Toxteth, Liverpool. A survey', *New Community*, IX: 344–53.

Ward, R.A. and Spitze, G. (1992) 'Consequences of parent–adult child coresidence. A review and research agenda', *Journal of Family Issues*, 13: 553–72.

Warr, P. (1987) *Unemployment and Mental Health*. Oxford: Oxford University Press.

Wearing, B. and Wearing, S. (1988) 'All in a day's leisure. Gender and the concept of leisure', *Leisure Studies*, 7: 111–23.

West, P. (1988) 'Inequalities? Social class differentials in health in British youth', *Social Science Medicine*, 27: 291–6.

West, P. (forthcoming) 'Health inequalities in the early years: Is there equalisation in youth?' *Social Science Medicine*.

West, P., Wight, D. and Macintyre, S. (1993) 'Heterosexual behaviour of 18-year-olds in the Glasgow area', *Journal of Adolescence*, 16: 367–96.

West, P. and Sweeting, H. (1996) 'Nae job, nae future. Young people and health in a context of unemployment', *Health and Social Care in the Community*, 4: 50–62.

Westwood, S. (1984) *All Day Every Day. Factory and Family in the Making of Women's Lives*. London: Pluto.

White, L. (1994) 'Coresidence and leaving home. Young adults and their parents', *Annual Review of Sociology*, 20: 81–102.

White, M. and McRae, S. (1989) *Young Adults and Long Term Unemployment*. London: Policy Studies Institute.

Widdicombe, S. and Woffitt, R. (1995) *The Language of Youth Subcultures. Social Identity and Action*. London: Harvester Wheatsheaf.

Wight, D. (1993) 'Constraint or cognition? Factors affecting young men's practice of safer heterosexual sex', in P. Aggleton, P. Davies and G. Hart (eds) *AIDS. Facing the Second Decade*. London: Falmer.

Willis, P. (1977) *Learning to Labour*. Farnbourgh: Saxon House.

Willis, P. (1990) *Common Culture*. Milton Keynes: Open University Press.

Willms, J.D. and Echols, F. (1992) 'Alert and inert clients. The Scottish experience of parental choice of schools', *Economic and Education Review*, 11: 339–50.

Woodroffe, C., Glickman, M., Barker, M. and Power, C. (1993) *Children, Teenagers and Health. Key Data*. Buckingham: Open University Press.

Wright, E.O. (1985) *Classes*. London: Verso.

Young, C.M. (1984) *Leaving Home and Returning Home. A Demographic Study of Young Adults in Australia*, Australian Family Research Conference Proceedings, Canberra, Vol. 1: 53–76.

Young, C.M. (1987) *Young People Leaving Home in Australia: The Trend Towards Independence*, Australian Family Formation Project Monograph, No. 9, Canberra.

Young, C.M. (1989) 'The effect of children returning home on the precision of the timing of the leaving-home stage', in E. Grebenik, C. Hohn and R. Mackensen (eds) *Later Phases of the Family Life Cycle. Demographic Aspects*. Oxford: Clarendon.

Young, J. (1971) *The Drugtakers. The Social Meaning of Drug Use*. London: Paladin.

Zinneker, J. (1990) 'What does the future hold? Youth and sociocultural change in the FRG', in L. Chisholm, P. Büchner, H.-H. Krüger and P. Brown (eds) *Childhood, Youth and Social Change. A Comparative Perspective*. London: Falmer.

Index

RE-STATING SOCIAL AND POLITICAL CHANGE
Colin Hay

Re-Stating Social and Political Change provides a critical introduction to the social, political and cultural changes that have occurred in Britain since the war, and argues that these changes can best be understood in terms of a theory of the state.

Re-Stating Social and Political Change reviews and assesses the major theories of the state that have sought to diagnose and explain the trajectories of Western societies. It provides a powerful case for the study of the state, and demonstrates how state theory can shed new light on war, social change, the extension of citizenship, the emergence of a patriarchal welfare state, the crisis of the state and the rise and demise of Thatcherism.

Features:
• focuses on 'real' examples from post-war British society
• makes considerable use of figures, tables and diagrams
• each chapter is structured around a key set of questions and issues
• a genuinely introductory critical account of existing theories.

Colin Hay has written a broad introduction to this pressing topic, which presents a new and distinctive argument about the role of the state in our understanding of social and political change. He also examines the impact of Thatcherism on the state, the possibility of a post-Thatcher settlement and the role of the current Labour party, and assesses the prognosis for the future.

Re-Stating Social and Political Change will be important reading for students of sociology, social and political theory, politics, social policy and women's studies.

Contents
Part 1: Stating the obvious – What is the state and why do we need it? – Part 2: Stating social and political change – War and social change – The sense of nonsense of consensus – Citizenship – Part 3: Re-stating crisis – Theories of state crisis – From contradiction to crisis – Part 4: Re-stating social and political change – Thatcherism – The state of the present – Bibliography – Index.

224pp   0 335 19386 2   (Paperback)   0 335 19387 0   (Hardback)

A SOCIOLOGY OF SEX AND SEXUALITY

Gail Hawkes

A Sociology of Sex and Sexuality offers a historical sociological analysis of ideas about expressions of sexual desire, combining both primary and secondary historical and theoretical material with original research and popular imagery in the contemporary context.

While some reference is made to the sexual ideology of Classical Antiquity and of early Christianity, the major focus of the book is on the development of ideas about sex and sexuality in the context of modernity. It questions the widespread assumption that the anxieties and fears associated with old sexual mores have been overcome in the late twentieth century context, and asks whether the discourses of Queer sexual politics have successfully fractured the binary categories of heterosexuality and homosexuality.

A Sociology of Sex and Sexuality will be of interest to students in the fields of sociology, sexual history, gender studies and cultural studies.

Contents
The specialness of sex – Sex and modernity – Enlightenment pleasures and bourgeois anxieties – The science of sex – Planning sex – Pleasurable sex – Liberalizing heterosexuality – Subverting heterosexuality – Final thoughts and questions – References – Index.

176pp   0 335 19316 1   (Paperback)   0 335 19317 X   (Hardback)